Keeping in Touch

KEEPING
IN TOUCH

Rosemary Harward

Keeping in Touch
Rosemary Harward

Published by Aspect Design, 2016

Designed, printed and bound by Aspect Design
89 Newtown Road, Malvern, Worcs. WR14 1PD
United Kingdom
Tel: 01684 561567
E-mail: allan@aspect-design.net
Website: www.aspect-design.net

ISBN 978-1-912078-72-1

In memory of Richard

List of Characters

Rosemary, author, born 1939.

Richard, husband, born 1937.

Brian, ex husband, born 1933 and father of:
Bryony, my daughter, born 1961.
Matthew, my son, born 1963.
Barnaby, my son, born 1969.
Natasha, my adopted daughter, born 1970.

Richard's children:
Belinda.
Sophie.
Nicola.
William, a.k.a. Will, Tashi.
All of whom lived with their mother, Penny.

Ann, my sister, and Jack, my brother-in-law.

Roy and Dulcie, my parents.

Dogs:
Badger, black Labrador cross.
Sirius, rough-haired Jack Russell.
Poppy, smooth-haired Jack Russell.
Puzzle, smooth-haired Jack Russell.
Seamus, red setter
Rufus, red setter.
various cats.

Introduction

We came to live at Windy Ridge in the summer of 1982, with Barnaby and Natasha. Bryony was at university and Matthew was living with his father. For six months we were unemployed and spent that time building an extension and were then taken on by the Manpower Services Commission Scheme and the National Trust in January 1983.

Windy Ridge cost us £34,000 and was a wooden bungalow with one small bedroom, one sitting room, a lean to bedroom, a passageway for a kitchen, and bathroom and a garage.

We knocked down the garage and incorporated it into the bungalow to make another bedroom and extended it at the back to provide a bigger kitchen and bathroom. It was on a main road with a fell behind it and had a wonderful view in front. We loved it dearly.

Windy Ridge
Skelwith Bridge
Ambleside
Cumbria

Christmas 1984

Dear ——

I hope you will forgive this duplicated letter. I did intend to write individually to everyone, but came to realise that this was an impossibility in the time. There may also be bits that you already know—but here goes on the saga of the Jones/Harward family.

We are ending the year in a much happier frame of mind than when we began it. Then all was insecurity and uncertainty. Richard's job with the Manpower Services Commission at the National Trust ended in January, and although he hadn't enjoyed it very much, the future did seem a rather horrid blank.

He decided to set up his own gardening service, under the Manpower Services Enterprise Allowance Scheme. Provided you had been unemployed for three months, or on one of their schemes, and that you could put £1,000 into the business, and that you were accepted onto the scheme, the government would pay you £40 a week for a year (taxable!) the intention of which was to get you off the ground. With the £1,000 Richard bought a second-hand van, which I sign-painted, and an answer phone.

Meanwhile, I was earning £45 a week for my three days a week with the National Trust, as volunteer co-ordinator, also on a Manpower Services Scheme. I was not enjoying my work very much, for various reasons. The people are very pleasant individually, but there were considerable frustrations and disillusions behind the scenes. Still, it was an interesting experience, and we made many contacts, and our knowledge of the Lake District increased enormously. We are still in touch, and one of our first jobs together for the Trust was to bring the vegetable garden at Hill Top (where Beatrix Potter lived) back into order as it was terribly overgrown.

You will gather that I have left the Trust. Half the point of these MSC schemes is to launch one into permanent work, and by Easter Richard had as much work as he could cope with, and I decided to join him. We had always wanted to work together, and as we had survived the building of the extension on Windy Ridge, we thought we could.

So one morning we went out knocking on doors for an hour, and have never had to knock on any more doors, or advertise, since. It is a very good area for gardening. There are many wealthy retired people up here, many hotels, many holiday houses, and very, very few flat gardens. We say we will do anything, and we have!

We had most of the tools in duplicate, and Richard had to buy a new chain saw to replace an old one, and we now have a good electric hedge-cutter. Sometimes we work together, sometimes apart, sometimes for a whole or half day, sometimes a one-off job or on a regular basis. Our customers vary as much as the work. Most of the work is very, very hard. It seems harder than farming—the equivalent of hay-making all the time, but we don't start until nine, and finish at five, mainly because we are often incapable of working another minute. We don't work at weekends either, which is marvellous.

The summer was fantastic! We didn't miss a single day because it never rained, but I was often reminded of the song 'Mad dogs and Englishmen go out in the midday sun,' as we toiled away with the temperature in the eighties. One person was so worried about us getting sunstroke she lent us her ancient straw hats. After one day when we had been dragging cut down trees and bushes onto a huge bonfire, we felt almost on fire with the heat, and at 5 pm we headed for the nearest shore of Windermere, threw off most of our clothes and sank gratefully into the cool water. The children swam nearly every day in the rivers.

We don't yet know whether we shall have enough work throughout the winter, but although the autumn has been extremely wet, it has been mild, and we have not been prevented from working more than two or three days. We were rather proud of ourselves on one day when we found we had kept going despite two inches of rain. At the moment we are very busy, and we have been offered decorating jobs for when the snow lies thick on the ground.

I am still hoping to get back into farming and we went to see several farms which were to let or for sale, but we simply have no hope of raising the capital, so we are starting in a very small way by renting two acres of land and a barn about three miles from here. I am going to keep a few sheep, and a couple of calves, and we hope to increase our land by renting other pieces. The trouble is that land is very scarce here, and snapped up by local farmers, whether it is good or poor. They survive only by means of the subsidies, and so are ever anxious to increase numbers of livestock.

However, in anticipation of the huge flock I *will* have, we bought a sheepdog puppy from Tim Longton, whom you may have seen on TV on *One Man and His Dog*. (We still have no telly.) Naturally this dog is the most amazing puppy in the world (to us) and I have already been teased by our neighbouring farmer who asks if it has gathered the fell yet.

Richard's setter Seamus was put down in the spring as he had a bad heart and could no longer walk as far as the gate without difficulty. Good old Badger went deaf (they were both thirteen) and as this was a worry in sheep country, Bryony took him off to Runcorn, where he is extremely happy. His nose is still in good working order, and believe me, there are many more enticing doggy smells in Runcorn than round here. She cycles and jogs, and he accompanies her, even to council meetings in the evenings, when she ties him up in the ladies until the meeting is finished. We still have Sirius and the two cats, and I persuaded Barnaby to keep hens for his Duke of Edinburgh Award. We bought an impractical trio of silver laced Wyandottes, and because we are not geared to livestock here and have no facilities, they caused us more bother than 150 cows. Very rapidly one went broody, and hatched out eight delightful chicks, and within days they were turning the garden into a waste land. We turned them onto the fell (alas without even consulting the farmer). When they grew large, they would not go to bed at night because they were afraid to pass their father, who sat at the entrance to the Ark, and we had to pluck them from trees and shrubs every night which got very boring. When they became edible, Richard solved most of the problems by killing the young cockerels, but unfortunately, in the dark he mistook one of the hens for a cock. As she hadn't laid an egg for months it was no great loss. We now have a proper henhouse, and to make the whole thing viable, I bought six hybrid hens, which lay eggs and don't go broody.

Bryony is enjoying her life in Runcorn, working hard, and because it is a small paper, she has to do a bit of everything, including being Aunty Bryony in the Children's Corner. She flits about the country at the weekends, visiting her numerous friends. She went to Corsica on a cross-country Tentrek holiday in the summer.

Matthew, in contrast, rarely travels, apart from to computer exhibitions and the like. He got himself a job with Atari, which seemed ideal and full of promise for him, but a month later the whole of his department was taken over and forty people were made redundant. He was shattered and so was I. He is now living with Brian in Bristol, and is hoping the firm will take him on again in some capacity. He has sold them one of his programmes for £300 (a week's work) and has various schemes afoot.

Barnaby and Natasha are doing well at school, despite the problems in a big comprehensive (a lot of stealing, smoking, lack of discipline, and a generally discouraging attitude towards those who want to work by the other pupils.

They are both keen on games, particularly Barnaby, and this means ferrying them after school and at weekends as the buses out here are infrequent and only go to Skelwith Bridge anyway. I am not a willing slave, and they bike and walk whenever possible.

Natasha is taller and a great deal more mature than Barnaby (physically) though she is a year younger. I am thinking of having a t-shirt printed with 'I am only fourteen' across the front. She is attractive, and this causes problems, as you can imagine.

We know we are in the backwoods up here (thank goodness) and have stepped off what some people call 'real life', but never more so than when our children visit us, usually with boyfriends (we put them in the old caravan—the little old stove is now working and the smoke from the chimney streams off across the valley—and no questions asked) and straight from university, and we try to look as if we meet pink hair, bleached hair, spiky hair, bangles, bracelets and beads (both sexes) and a stunning assortment of clothes, every day.

I finished typing my book on my first year at Bowood, but it keeps coming back from the publishers. A pity, because I *still* think it's good. I want to illustrate it myself, but perhaps I'll never get the chance. However, I've done it, and like Elgar when he'd finished writing *The Dream of Gerontius* (comparisons *are* odious) I could have written on it, 'This is the best of me.' It was the most significant year of my life.

Well, I hope you will have gathered from all this that we are well, cheerful, hopeful and happy, and actually *surviving*. Long may it last.

And the same to you,

Love from us all.

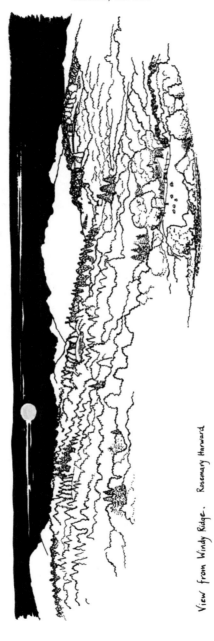

View from Windy Ridge.   Rosemary Harward

Windy Ridge

8 December 1985

Dear ——

As my normal letter writing has practically come to a full stop this year, I am once again resorting to a duplicated letter. Apologies.

Grassroots Gardening continues to flourish, and Grassroots Farming is off the ground. We have had a really happy year, full of interest and variety. Our fears that we might have no work during last winter were unfounded, and in fact our much looked-forward to 'rest' period never happened. The good thing about winter is that one is forced to stop working earlier because it gets dark! The money I had managed to set aside for these no-work days therefore went into our farming, and so far the bottomless pit has sucked in over £2,500.

We gave ourselves the whole of Christmas week off last year, and completed the fencing of the two-acre field and barn we had rented for five elderly Rough Fell ewes. We intended to sell them off after their crop of lambs, but got rather fond of them, so they are still with us. We also bought two cheap Hereford cross calves at Kendal market and were initiated into the luck money system. On buying them, I was surprised when a farmer came up to me and thrust a pound into my hand and said, 'She's a good 'un.' He was right. As the barn is three and a half miles away, and we had to go twice a day to feed them, you can see why our farming is not an economical venture. On one occasion, snow fell so heavily we couldn't get the van out, so I walked there and back with the milk powder and flask of hot water on my back. There is no light or water laid on. It's all a bit primitive.

The sheep, despite having hardly any teeth, awful feet, and being used as practice material by the dog, throve and produced eight marvellous lambs. They are purebred (though not pedigree);

we kept the female lambs, and are eating the males. It is voted the best lamb tasted for years by everyone. Meanwhile, we were offered another field, even further away, with magnificent views, but difficult access. We took it on in some trepidation as we couldn't see how we would get the sheep onto it, let alone out of it. Again we had to fence it for the equivalent of three years' rent. A neighbouring farmer offered us the use of his dip, and even fetched the sheep with his dog as mine was not then capable of doing anything but scattering them! We bought fifteen hoggs (young maiden sheep) and then Richard decided we needed transport for them, so he bought a vintage tractor for £400 with cab—a little old grey Ferguson.

He drove it thirty miles home from Shap, downhill nearly all the way and fortunately its brakes still worked.

I have been on several Agricultural Training Board courses, including a sheep-shearing course, which was held rather late and I had already done mine by hand. It takes a farmer about a minute to do a sheep, it took me an hour, and that was with Richard pinning parts of it down at times. My poor back. Rough Pells have really magnificent fleeces (which was what attracted me to them), but I got an average of £2 a fleece from the Wool Marketing Board, so you can see the returns are not rolling in.

Thirty-four inches of rain fell during July, August and September, but the weather did not get us down until we heard that the ground was cracking with the drought in the south. It was dreary going out day after day in our waterproofs, which are so cumbersome. A lot of our work in the summer is mowing lawns and somehow we carried on. Richard mowed one large lawn in a terrific thunderstorm one day because we were going on holiday the next week and couldn't put it off.

The only week we could get away was after Barnaby's exams— he got eight O levels—and before Natasha's German exchange friend arrived (I vowed it was the last afterwards). We left the children in charge of the house, etc. and took off to the Outer

Hebrides for ten days of camping in the loneliest and most remote places we could find. It was bliss, and though the weather was more atmospheric than sunny, compared to later on in the summer it was good. Up there it is hard to believe one is in the same country as Salisbury Cathedral, Sainsburys and *Star Wars*. I have never been on such beautiful and pure beaches, but I would like to have seen the country before all the horrid little bungalows were built and all the electricity wires were strung over the scenery. We saw an elderly woman milking her cow by the road, and had an interesting chat on housecows and their management.

Since Christmas I have done several drawings in pen and ink for customers, of houses or hotels. I have really enjoyed doing them as it makes a contrast from the physical work of gardening. Some of our jobs have been *really* enjoyable. To take £400 to the garden centre (and we have an excellent one in Ambleside) and spend it on plants of our choice and then plant them, is one example. I also had the chance to redesign an hotel garden of an acre and then we carried out the work and planted it up.

Recently, we had to fell five eighty-foot-tall sycamore trees which were in a place surrounded by other trees and shrubs. That got the adrenalin going. We managed not to smash anything other than a small rhododendron.

Then, and most exciting of all, at the end of October, our favourite customer gave us the use of her land. Most of it is very rough, and so wild that a herd of red deer live on it, but about ten of the seventy acres is fenced and runs down to the lake of Grasmere, and must be one of the loveliest places in the Lake District. This is three and a half miles in another direction!

This brings me to Moss, the wonder dog, who is supposed to control the sheep on all this land. We are being trained at the moment by an expert, and go once a fortnight to a class on a local farm. I was told last week that he is really a man's dog (huh?) being what they call a 'strong' dog, in other words, very wilful and incredibly keen when he sees the sheep. We have a long way to go, but he is getting better. It's not as easy as it looks, and as the shepherd says, he's really training me, not the dog.

Now we are into tupping. Our tup (or ram as I used to call them) was given to us by a farmer. 'He's nowt to look at, but by God, he's a good tup,' he said. Rhyme the *u* with c*oo*k and you get the flavour better. He's so old his horns have had to be cut off, but he's tame and stands quite still to be raddled or marked with paint so we can tell which ewes he's served, which I appreciate.

All has not gone smoothly. Two of our three calves we bought recently, died. The post mortem revealed that one was just very bad luck. It had choked on regurgitated food. The vet thought that the other one had died because it had not had the colostrum from its mother and had succumbed to infection. More than £100 down the drain, as well as the emotional upset.

Bryony, now twenty-four, is still in Runcorn on the newspaper. She failed her proficiency test which surprised us all and was a serious setback to her getting out of Runcorn, but she took it again and awaits the results after Christmas. She went to Russia with Brian for a holiday, and has acquired a Lancia. It is old, but in very good condition (it belonged to our favourite customer) and had done only thirty thousand miles. She is going to car maintenance classes to keep down the cost of keeping it.

Matthew, who was unemployed last Christmas, landed on his feet, and is working very happily at Bath University on computer programming. He has also invented a programme and is getting royalties for that, and writes here and in America for computer magazines. We talk unintelligibly to each other, more a sort of sign language. Brian persuaded him to move out of his flat eventually, and he headed straight for the more salubrious area of Bath and got himself a small but pleasant flat on the top floor of a Georgian house and spent nothing on it but a wall to wall computer. I bought him a saucepan for his birthday. I don't think he had noticed he hadn't got one.

Barnaby is enjoying the privileges of the sixth form and is a prefect. He was given a badge, but sadly and indicatively, will not wear it. They are allowed to wear whatever they like and I was rather shocked at his initial choice until I saw his mates in string vests and multicoloured hair, and realised he was only trying to fit in. Basically, he is fairly conventional. He has a guinea pig of which he is rather fond. To keep it company he bought another. Guess what? We have had a guinea pig population explosion. Teenage guinea pigs never have more than one or two babies. His had five the first time and seven the second. There are now sixty miles between the pair, which I hope to make a permanent arrangement.

We have had what can only be described as a turbulent year with Natasha. I now sympathise with all parents who have suffered teenage problems. Why there isn't more teenage battering I can't imagine. Probably because most of them are bigger than their parents. I love to hear of anyone who has undergone the agonies (particularly if they are in the past and have therefore somehow survived). However, at the moment she is much happier as her current boyfriend is a twenty-one-year-old Italian with a car and an earring (her description when she told me.) But am I?

Brian has suggested that she spends the sixth form years with him. Yes, please. I'm just afraid she'll change her mind!

We do think of other things beside sheep occasionally, and have as good a social life as we desire, and sometimes go to concerts, the cinema, etc. We're holding out against the dreaded telly. I do regret missing some programmes and the children feel they will be warped for ever, but I know it would be nothing but an area of conflict in this tiny house, and meanwhile the long winter evenings seem to be flying by without it.

Love from us all and a very happy Christmas.

Let the wealthy and great roll in splendour and state –
I envy them not I declare it.
I eat my own lamb, my own chicken and ham,
I shear my own fleece and I wear it.
I have lawns I have bowers
I have fruits I have flowers,
The lark is my morning alarmer.
So jolly boys now here's God speed the plough
Long life
and success
to the farmer!

ANON

Rosemary Harward

Windy Ridge

5 December 1986

Dear ——

Where to start?

Nineteen eighty-six started, or rather continued, with problems with Natasha, which became very severe until one awful night when she went right off the rails and disappeared and I went to the police as I thought she had gone into the mountains to commit suicide—actually she had hitched eight miles to Windermere at 1 am and was with a boy! Not until the police had first searched in the loft and looked in the freezer (yes, for her body) did she turn up at the school, who were by then involved also.

After that we went through a long and terrible time when we did know exactly where she was because she had no freedom at all of the kind she had always enjoyed. The police were very supportive and helped me to cut her off from the company she had been in. We went to the doctor, social worker and psychiatrist in order to help both her and ourselves. The psychiatrist was very deaf and smoked like a chimney in a building which had 'no smoking' notices on every wall. He said he never saw children on their own as he found they always led him up the garden path!

Eventually, she took her O levels and got nine, mostly As and Bs. She said she didn't deserve them as she hadn't done any work. As Brian's offer to have her for the sixth form years still stood, it seemed the best thing for us all for her to live with him. She and I were sadly locked in a no-trust situation on both sides, and time and distance seemed the only way to soften that.

I think she has been much happier with Brian and likes the school in Bristol, has made masses of friends and seems to be doing well. She is embarking on things like the Ten Tors Walk which makes me smile. She came up here for half term, behaved like a model daughter, had one of her boyfriends to stay (a nice lad, but already in the past) cooked us a delicious meal—she is now a vegetarian which Brian finds a pity as he is now a dab hand at lovely casseroles—and she is at last sixteen.

While we were in the throes of this muddle and unhappiness, William, Richard's son, said he would like to come and stay with us after his A levels and earn some money up here. For the first time in my life, I felt I simply could not cope with anyone extra, though I could see it was very important for him to come and live with Richard. However, as Natasha was departing for the south, we said he was very welcome after she had gone. We did, in fact, have a breathing space of a few weeks before William arrived, full of keenness to start his independent leaving-school life, only to find that in getting a job at a pub three miles round the fell, and living with us on a working rather than a holiday basis, was a much more disciplined and rigid regime than he had had before.

Within a week he had had an accident on Natasha's bike—his only means of transport—and cut his hand to the bone cycling home at 1 am without lights. Shortly after that he had another accident and wrote Natasha's bike off, but did no damage to himself. Barnaby was understandably reluctant to lend him his own only means of transport, but was persuaded after a couple of days. From then on the word *bike* became a really dirty word, and as Richard said, the garden became strewn with bits of broken bicycle; this was an exaggeration, but Barnaby now has a brand new bike from the insurance.

We had had images of walking with William (he is really keen on the hills), sailing with William, taking William to Hadrian's Wall, Yorkshire, etc., and reluctantly, but necessarily, driving with William as he is taking his test in December. At the end of two and a half months we had done none of these things. His times off never coincided with ours, and as he was never told when his next day off was, we couldn't plan ahead and arrange a day off with him. Many days we never saw him. He got up after we had left and got in when we were in bed. It was highly unsatisfactory, and also very sad. The good thing was that he saved up enough to get to India, which is his primary object during his year out. In the times we did see him we felt very out of touch with how young people feel, think, and act these days. We had a splendid, lively last weekend with him when his sisters Sophie and Nicola came up and got him organised for the interview he had to have in London re. his Indian trip. They persuaded him to spend some of his miser's hoard on a pair of decent trousers. The ones he was most fond of were a pair Richard wore on the farm 20 years ago, complete with original diesel stains and real fly buttons, which kept coming open.

He sailed through the interview, but fell on the escalator, ruined his new trousers and had to have four stitches in his leg . . .

While we're on the subject of children, Bryony failed her proficiency test three times and finally decided to try for another job without it. Within a fortnight she had got one as district reporter for a Telford paper based in Whitchurch, Shropshire, at twice the salary and with car provided. Her excitement was marred by her boyfriend refusing to have a commuting relationship and so ending it. When they visited us, he had produced a carrier bag full of bottles of wine and cans of beer which I thought was most civil of him. That is, until he very speedily snapped open the first can and drank it before I could reach for the glasses, and proceeded to knock off cans and bottles independently of us throughout the weekend. We got our revenge, however, because on the Saturday morning a load of hay was delivered, and all hands were called out of bed to unload it at Grasmere. I honestly forgot that he had hay fever. Once we had adjusted to his being a fluent anarchist, we rather liked him, and respected his ability to teach deprived children in Runcorn, and when he was openly touched by his first experience of holding a lamb, we thought he must be all right.

Bryony wrote a very happy letter last week. She is hoping to buy a house, have a cat, and she's got a new boyfriend. Hurray!

Matthew gave up his job at the university (Bath)—my jaw has

dropped a number of times this year—as he had so much freelance work on. I suppose he knows what he is doing. He has a marvellous girlfriend, an Australian girl who has a history degree and who has come to Europe to see the history.

She is the same age as Matthew, twenty-two. During the whole of her visit we battled with atrocious inferiority feelings as she has done and seen everything we have done or seen, only more so, and more. Her knowledge of sheep was extensive as she had worked on a sheep ranch. When she asked how many we had I felt a bit foolish saying forty-nine. She has dived on the Great Reef, skied in the Himalayas, lived all over the world, and had even heard of and could discuss intimately with my father about some obscure mediaeval French tribe that he was studying. She is also blond, pretty and has a super figure. We had a lovely weekend, it was touching and charming to see young people in love. We climbed Helm Crag, a mini mountain, and had a barbecue on our land at Grasmere, a perfect setting, and Fran persuaded Matthew to take her out for a row on the lake. The weather was idyllic. She has introduced Matthew to *culture* and even took him to Greece. Amazing.

In true Matthew fashion, as soon as he gave up his job he moved, this time to an even more salubrious address in Bath, where they are in Connaught Mansions, albeit the top floor. The place is so affluent and security conscious that you can't even get in to ring the bell after 10 pm.

Barnaby, even-tempered, sensible and completely unflappable, even when he ought to be, is taking A levels this year. He's taking religious studies and has recently been to Israel. For this he needed £500, so he worked with us all through the holidays. When we all went out together he had to be packed into the back of the van with the tools, and was sometimes found fast asleep on the journey home.

So it's not just the over forties who find the work exhausting. We were amused on one occasion when William asked us why we didn't go walking after work. He said it was just a question of mind over matter. Barnaby, for once arguing on our side, he usually takes the opposite point of view as a matter of principle, explained that it was *not* so, one was *really* tired. It was unfortunate that there was not enough work for William in Grassroots too.

Going back to the spring, we had an awful lambing. The ewes were over at Grasmere, miles away, the weather was bitterly cold with a fiendish northeast wind. We had five old originals and fifteen inexperienced maidens. At the height of lambing I was going over four times a day and for weeks I got up before six and went over before breakfast and last thing at night. We put the sheep in and out of the barn; milked them for the weakly lambs; held the flighty ones; buried endless bodies (lambs); used the car as an emergency ambulance to the vets and as a delivery room when we got there (it still has an unusual odour about it); and emerged from the experience bloody and almost bowed. The only thing that cheered me was that all the 'real' farmers around were having a similar time, and we swapped grim stories as we passed, bleary eyed, in the dawn.

Eager to repeat these horrors we bought ten more young sheep this autumn to build up the flock, which we have now registered. Instead of sending our two heifers off for meat as intended, we have put them in calf as the founders of our suckler herd. So our returns will be delayed at least two years. The three Angus/Friesian heifers are now a year old and thriving. It has taken me all year to save up enough to pay for all the hay that will be eaten this winter. We had enough grass to make hay, but had no equipment and no intention of making any this year. But we have now bought an old mower, chain harrow, transport box, and cattle hayrack at local farm sales this autumn. These are the reasons *we* haven't been to Greece.

We headed for Scotland again in the summer and made pilgrimages to Gavin Maxwell's home, where he wrote *Ring of Bright Water*, and to Frank Fraser Darling's Island Farm on the Summer Isles. We camped in remote and beautiful places and the only difficult decisions were whether to move on and see more, or stay put and soak up the sun which shone all day and nearly all night. It could not have been more perfect.

Grassroots keeps us going very well. Some of it is interesting, some of it is very boring. At the end of the autumn, we decided to cut down our earning days to four, as we hadn't walked anywhere for months and had been continuously and arduously busy even through that lovely weather in September. So we now have a definite farming day—dipping, dosing, fencing, walling, etc. (no money, but nice)—four gardening days, one walking/getting out day, and one vital day sorting out at home. We'd really like a little but profitable farm, but how? Is there such a thing? It seems increasingly doubtful. Meanwhile, Moss and I keep practising for when we have a few hundred sheep. Even Sirius is still incredibly fit, and recently managed a mountain and twelve miles on her six-inch, thirteen-year-old legs.

To fill in any gaps in the evenings, we have joined the Grasmere Players, not to act, but to participate in other ways, and we are enjoying this very much.

It's ideal for the winter. They are putting on a play just before Christmas and I am wondering how I am going to fit in all the preparations for a family Christmas (my turn this year) as well as the rehearsals and performances.

Have a very happy Christmas and a prosperous new year,
Love from us all.

Happy is the man with the intellect to follow Newton's philosophy, but happy too is he who knows the secrets of the countryside, the art of gardening, the soils favoured by the different plants, the water and the situations they need. Let no man despise so humble a pursuit, it is one of the cares and interests of God himself.

INSCRIPTION ON WINDOWPANE IN MONTACUTE HOUSE. DATED 1770.

Bank House Farm
Silverdale
Camforth
Lancashire

December 1987

Dear ——

Well, miracles do happen, and another one has happened to me. We're farmers and farming an idyllic little farm on the shores of Morecambe Bay, back in Lancashire where I came from (and swore never to return) and what's more, we still have a leg in the Lakes as Windy Ridge is still ours. How did all this good fortune come about?

I wrote last year that we were getting restless, our sheep and cattle were growing in number and taking more time, yet the gardening was growing no less, and I felt increasingly that I could not spend the rest of my life with my head nearer the ground than my rear end. We survived the winter with a few dodgy periods, but decorating helped us through until April, when lambing went very well. I saw only one lamb born, did not have to help any ewes, and all the lambs survived—thirty-three this year. Our two heifers calved, but one calf was born dead, very disappointing indeed and I had to buy a calf from a farmer for £80 which the bereaved mother took to with some suspicion and a lot of supervision.

About this time, various farms came on the market and we spent a lot of time working out budgets and speculating (vainly as we had no hope of buying!) Strangely, when we saw an advert in the local paper for the short term tenancy and part-time wardening of a National Trust farm we did not bother applying. It all seemed so temporary. By chance, a good friend of ours who is a National Trust Warden passed by one day, and said, 'Why don't you apply— it would just suit you?'

We sent for the details and I had one of my brainstorms as I read them—it was really us, the NT even wanted keen gardeners as the previous tenant who had died had kept the yard and garden full of flowers. Then followed a very frantic time as deadlines were close: visits to the bank manager, detailed budgets drawn up for three years, official viewing day with what seemed like hundreds of other candidates, and finally the very official interview where we knew everyone on the panel by their first name, including Richard's former boss, with whom Richard had not been at all happy, but who was very nice indeed on this occasion! Then suddenly the farm was ours, and Richard had to be here by the beginning of June!

We sold Grassroots Gardening to an ideal young couple for £1,000, so we did not have to let any of our customers down. However, they could not take it over immediately so I carried on with spasmodic help from Richard and Barnaby until the end of June when Barnaby had finished his exams. I moved here, Barnaby began an independent existence at Windy Ridge, part gardening (to help the new people) and partly in the cafe attached to Brantwood at Coniston for the holidays.

Richard started life here camping on a bed he found in the outbuildings, and as we were leaving most of the furniture at Windy Ridge as a holiday cottage, it was back to orange boxes and bare floors. It's surprising where furniture comes from when you have nothing, and what we have now is very adequate. Making it actually look nice is what I enjoy doing next to farming, and I have a long way to go.

Richard began to buy second hand machinery for the forty acres of hay we had to make in July. The farm had not been grazed since the winter.

The farm is fifty minutes drive from Windy Ridge, through lovely scenery all the way. We have fifty-seven acres of grassland in a designated Area of Outstanding Natural Beauty. It is a traditional farm with a natural Limestone yard, early eighteenth-century house and buildings, byres, barns etc., and small fields divided by limestone walls and quickthorn hedges. It is almost in the centre of

Silverdale, but with its back to the village so that it is very private and quiet. The fields spread down to the shore of the bay, where the limestone cliffs drop to the remarkable salt marshes, where we have grazing rights, and which occasionally get completely covered by high tides. The fields are full of flowers including one with orchids and banks of wild thyme and there are a lot of retired naturalists in the area who keep a beady eye on them! Richard wardens two and a half days a week in various Trust-owned areas around here, mainly woodland which again are renowned for their flora and fauna, butterflies, etc.

We intended to farm organically, but there are a number of restrictions such as no vaccinating or routine worming of sheep, which we think is nonsense, so at present we aim to farm in an old-fashioned way with no artificial fertilisers or sprays, and all the animals will be reared as naturally as possible, without the use of feed additives and growth promoters, hormone implants, etc. We need to find a market for the end product as there is not much point in all that if you send the animal to a market where we do not know what happens to the poor thing, and no one knows it should be worth more money.

We have 120 breeding ewes, twenty followers, and we will have twelve suckler cows, some of which are still young things at the moment. We have bought two hundred point of lay pullets and they are in three super new hen houses out on the fields, where they should be fertilising as they go and we move the houses every week.

We are selling the eggs at the farm door and at a local shop, and so far have not had to smash any, though I do have nightmares of mountains of eggs that nobody wants. These are *real* free range. We discovered when we went on a poultry course that the Big Boys have moved in on the free range egg market to get more money, and most of them are no more free range than Deep Litter. They recommend one pophole to a thousand hens. It would take all day to get out if you were at the back of the queue. We don't have yolk colourant in the food either, which some people have commented on. I hope we manage to keep our nerve on this one as the yolks are at the moment a pretty yellow and not a deep orange. We also have three charming young pigs, Boadicea, Brittania, and Black Eyed Susan. They were meant for our freezer and other people's, but it was fatal to get females. I don't seem to have problems sending males to slaughter, but potential *mothers* are a different matter.

We inherited five peacocks and a few guinea fowl which are merely ornaments, but the other enterprises may be viable in three years time. Meanwhile, we are letting Windy Ridge and this is going very well so far. We hope people will come in the winter as it is so warm and cosy. It is let right over Christmas and the New Year, and people do appear to be very pleased with it. I go up to the Lakes twice a week, once to clean, etc. Windy Ridge, and I also still do some gardening as we have retained the land at Grasmere. Richard goes up once a week to garden at Grasmere also. Life is a little complicated sometimes (slight understatement) but it seems to be working.

Getting the house completely redecorated has taken second place to setting up the farming, but I have managed to get the kitchen more to my taste, and make one room sittable in. We discovered the original old fireplace behind three more modern ones. We have found that wardening is a very sociable occupation and we are always meeting new people and there are always meetings of local committees, visits by NT botanists and conservationists, and this month we had the complete National Trust Regional Committee here for coffee and a tour of the farm, after which they took us out for lunch which we thoroughly enjoyed.

We are fortunate in our 'boss'—the agent of the farm—is actually the director of the north west region, Laurence Harwood (spelt differently) whom we have always liked, and he comes down about once a month to discuss various matters, projects ,etc., and we then go to see what's happening on the properties, about the only time I get off the farm for pleasure.

Brief news of the children—Bryony is happy on the *Shropshire*

Star—still failing her proficiency test inexplicably, but settled in to her first little house complete with cat and home-made pond. Matthew has just moved to Glasgow University with his girlfriend Fran, both of whom are working on the Strategic Decision Support Research Unit with Colin Eden, an old friend of ours who is now a professor. Barnaby managed to get four A levels and so is now a student at London University at the School of Oriental and African Studies, reading Religious Studies and History—a somewhat unusual choice which I think made it easier for him to get a place than if he had chosen English, for example. I confess I did want him to go to London, and his hall of residence is very near to where I was in Bloomsbury, though student life appears to be rather different now. He has a girlfriend at Carlisle College of Art, and considers himself to be 'committed', which in these days of AIDS can be no bad thing at his age.

I saw Natasha very recently in Bath, after almost a year, and time *has* done wonders. She is, at seventeen, completely independent of both Brian and me, both financially and apparently emotionally. Brian had an equally stormy year with her, and eventually withdrew her from school before she was expelled for truancy.

She also held a party in his flat in his absence, which was gatecrashed with appalling results, and which he is still seething about. Having well and truly antagonised him, she found a flat of her own, and a job, and seems to be surviving with lots of friends, money, and, I hope, happiness. She looked quite stunning and has been modelling clothes at a £100 a time.

One of Richard's children is working in America, one studying in Mannheim, one in love with a forty-eight-year-old trombonist and hoping to work in the foreign office, and one at Nottingham University. As all the children hitch, hike, bike, bus, or drive up to see us, we don't lack visitors either.

Re-reading this letter I can see why I have felt pretty much submerged this year and have had no time to read, write, bake, hang curtains other than with drawing pins, train sheepdogs (we now have two) or join the WI.

We wish you a very Happy Christmas and are very happy to say that dreams do come true, however long or short they last.

And do remember that Bank House Farm is only four miles away from the motorway Junction at Camforth on the M6, and we'd love to see you!

Love from us both.

Bank House Farm

Rosemary Harward

Bank House Farm

Christmas 1988

Dear ——

Looking back over this year's engagement diary, the most noticeable entries are the astonishing numbers of visitors we have had and the number of times we have done the sheep's feet. As well as local friends and relatives, we have had people from far flung places (like Wiltshire), school visits, playgroup visits, National Trust VIPs and committee meetings, organic inspection visits, the bank manager (twice!), a farm walk, and, of course, children and parents. No wonder the curtains are *still* hanging by drawing pins, and the only reason the house is now decorated completely is because Barnaby came home during the summer desperate for money, and we paid him to paint almost the whole of the upstairs, which suited him because he had the freedom to gad about the country in between. William came for a week in similar financial plight and did some really filthy jobs like scraping off the bit of panelling we uncovered, and removing the paint and cement stains from the tiles in the living room, thus making another huge leap forward to interior civilisation.

Lambing was a shattering experience and for nearly six weeks we did not leave the farm together. Our lambing per cent was good for the Rough Fells and we had a lot of twins and no ewes succumbed at birth, though we did have a few 'pet lambs' from triplets and rejects. Selling the breeding lambs was very disappointing. We think our expectations were too high, prices were lower than last year, and our place on the market ballot system too low. We hope to gain the Organic Soil Association Symbol by next year and may be able to negotiate direct with other organic farms for the female lambs, and with a local high-class supermarket for the males, and so cut the market out altogether. I hate seeing my sheep in the market.

We had five good bull calves, one of which we sold as a store for £400 this autumn. The others are still with their mothers, for the winter at least. So during the summer we had three hundred head of sheep, and a little herd of five cows and their calves, and these were running with eight heifers and a borrowed Aberdeen Angus bull. We bought another ten heifers (£3,500 worth) for the winter, so the cowshed is full again.

With some trepidation, we drove the sheep onto the salt marshes in the summer, and discovered that our sheep don't mix with the other sheep out there that also have grazing rights, and they tend to come back on the farm at night. It does mean walking miles to get in stragglers when you want them in, to do their feet for example, or because there is a high tide due, and to 'look' them every day, but the grazing was excellent, and so far we have had no drownings or dog troubles.

The pigs have been a great success—except financially— farrowing within a day of each other, in brand new pig arcs that only arrived as one was in labour and which was assembled at incredible speed and in desperation in the dark. As it was their first litter, we didn't know what to expect, but *they* remained perfectly calm and fifteen piglets survived. Four died despite the kiss of life (well, *I'm* not squeamish), and after providing endless entertainment in the field, eleven went to market where the contrast between our outdoor reared, firm, pink, confident pigs, and the flabby, pale, anaemic blobs that had come out of sheds, etc. was remarkable. The other four, destined for Ashdown Smokers exclusive bacon are still enjoying the Great Outdoors for a while longer. Having your own bacon and eggs, ham, beef and lamb is an achievement, but I think I'll go vegetarian when we retire—I don't like the way most animals are fed and reared.

We had a holiday! Marvellous farming friends offered to take over. How could we refuse what might be the last holiday in years? It was at least two years since we had a day off, and it had to fit in with lambing, calving, dipping, clipping, haymaking and, of course, Windy Ridge changeover day. There seemed to be only one possible week, we fixed it for the last week in June, and we planned to start haymaking the day after our return. Unfortunately, the weather turned fine the week before we left. Perfect haytiming weather day after day. Richard became more and more gloomy and fretful. All the local farmers were out until dark, cutting and tedding. We departed for Scotland after I had taken full responsibility for so doing! We did have a superb holiday in Arran, camping in fields surrounded by haymakers, which we carefully avoided mentioning, but you will remember (how can we ever forget?) that the weather broke the first week in July, and apart from being the laughing stock of the local farming community, we had a very fraught time getting the hay in. I still think it was worth it.

Our first NT cum Bank House Farm walk was in August, on a scorchingly hot day. Eighty people came, of all ages, and they were taken on a guided tour of the farm. Richard gave a demonstration on sheep's feet—what else?—and I gave one on sheepdog handling, showing a trained dog, Moss, working; then an untrained one, Dan, having a go. I prayed there would be a difference! But one man was so impressed by the empathy he imagined between Moss and myself that he wrote an article on us—so far unaccepted. Friends then served cups of tea and cream scones as people filed in at the front door and out at the back. Barnaby collected the money as they went in. I seem to remember he was wearing the most amazing pair of shorts and hairstyle that day.

I could write a treatise on egg production, but my conclusion would still be: a complete mystery. There seems to be no pattern to people's egg buying, and now just as we have built up a quality product and have actually expanded and bought another henhouse, the media put on a programme about salmonella in eggs and blew it out of all proportion. We shall continue to have a boiled egg—not hard—for breakfast every day, and if I had time to bake I would be making hundreds of meringues. Things must be improving as this year I have baked the Christmas cake. It is the first cake I have baked since coming to Bank House. It's a bit frustrating having all these eggs and not using them, as you can imagine.

Windy Ridge has been occupied by visitors almost all the year round and is a vital part of our income. We haven't had any problems except the drains blocking up a few times due to people not obeying the instructions. Clearing drains has got to be a speciality of mine. I enjoy going up to the Lake District every week, although it is a hectic day, as I have to get up early to do the usual chores before I set off. I deliver a large boxful of eggs to the National Trust office in Ambleside, who are good customers, and I zip over to Grasmere to deliver more eggs and to see our animals when they are there, then garden and house at Windy Ridge, shopping on the way home, animals when I get back if Richard hasn't managed to do them, and, finally, a well-deserved whisky before making the meal.

Richard goes up to Grasmere to work at The Wyke every week, and he continues to enjoy the wardening which is very varied work. He went away on a five-day woodland management course to Derbyshire in October, all paid for by the Trust. I had my turn off for one night when Barnaby returned to London where he and four other students are paying £9,000 for a rented house for one year. He drove down with the car crammed with cast off furniture, bedding, food, etc. The car is eleven years old and having done 150,000 miles is not now capable of doing more than sixty mph. Before Richard visited William at Nottingham University, he filled in the holes with Polyfilla and sprayed them. The car now looks like an army camouflage target, but the Polyfilla stayed put. We are rather dreading having to send it to the knackers, it's so much a part of the family.

Natasha remains at a distance in Bristol, Matthew happy in Glasgow, Barnaby ditto in London, Bryony the same in Shropshire. Belinda is engaged to a young man and is getting married in April.

We have now seen the whole cycle round, and we should know

what to expect at all the varying seasons of the year. The only unknown factor is the weather and the number of walls which will fall down next year. It should get easier and we hope we will have a bit more time to 'stand and stare'. Even half an hour would be nice!

A very happy Christmas and love from us both.

Birds in tree at night, front yard at Bank House Farm

Bank House Farm

Christmas 1989

Dear ——

This has been the year of the fiftieth birthday—*mine!* To celebrate I had a party, the first for years. Seven out of the eight children, accompanied by girlfriends/boyfriends/husband were able to come. I planned a barbecue, which I'd never had in my life before, and we had no contingency plans if it rained due to hay and straw in all the barns. I didn't have time to worry about it and happily it was an idyllic evening, sunny, calm and warm. About fifty people came, and to tell the truth, I remember very little about anything but a very splendid sunset over Morecambe Bay and the farm, and how happy I was.

And I swear I didn't drink more than one glass of wine!

That night there were young people sleeping in beds, sheds and barns. Nobody had to rush off the next morning and we had a lovely family gathering, eating left overs and talking and sprawling about in the hot sunshine.

My birthday presents included a whole litter of Gloucester Old Spot pigs made as soft toys by Bryony and a wonderful clockwork pig from Barnaby, which grunts and wiggles its nose and tail. I also got an Ayrshire calf—real—from Matthew, Fran and Bryony and a real goat from my sister along with some guinea fowl from Richard's sister. Apart from the hens we now have five geese, three Norfolk Black turkeys, three ducks, eight bantams and two fantail pigeons. The peacocks increased to eight and the Silkie hens multiply inordinately all summer long. And, of course, the four cats and three dogs. I appear to be indulging to the full my passion for animals, but perhaps I'm going into overkill so that when we retire from here I shall be utterly content with a budgie or possibly a hamster.

Sirius the Jack Russell is sixteen, going on seventeen, she looks exceedingly old and tottery, but is still able to home in on the cats' food like a torpedo when no one is looking.

Just after I had sent off my letter last year we were awarded the Soil Association Symbol for the farm, and we are now gaining confidence in our ability to cope without herbicides, pesticides, fungicides and artificial fertilizers. Our animals have survived and even look well. Because the 'organic' publicity in the media has been so great, and because public awareness has increased about what awful things do happen in the farming and food industry, the National Trust is thinking of making many more of its farms organic. So we have found ourselves, inexperienced as we are, rather in the forefront, and have even had the director general, Angus Stirling, here. We were asked to write an article on what it means to go organic—which we wrote in a tent on a Scottish island with a glass of Islay Mist in one hand and a pen in the other—no wonder the words flowed so fluently!

Not all enterprises need to be organic even when the farm is. The hens and pigs cannot be, because we cannot buy in organically produced food for them, although they have additive and hormone-free food.

The cows and sheep go as organic beef and lamb to a local supermarket and we get a 10 per cent premium on the price. This is a very simple method of selling and eliminated the market and is almost free of stress and terror for the animals. There is a huge demand for organic meat. We have been asked if we do refrigerated transport to London, Liverpool and Manchester, and when Booths asked us how many lambs we had and we replied, 'About 120,' the buyer said, '120 a week?' Ha!

Our time off increased this year to eight blissful, peaceful days on the islands of Islay and Jura in June (touring all the whisky distilleries) thanks to Sheila and Philip, who once again took over with such brilliant competence that not once did any worry cross my mind while we were away. We have also spent three nights away at organic events. I went down to Bryony's for the weekend of Mothering Sunday and was well and truly spoiled. I spent a weekend very enjoyably in Glasgow with Matthew and Fran, and Richard went south for Belinda's wedding in May. It was impossible for us both to leave the farm at that time of the yea unfortunately. I am trying to persuade Richard that we need some sort of regular time off, even if it's once a fortnight, but there is always so much to do.

Haymaking was slightly less traumatic this year. We came home from holiday all raring to go, to find a few frizzled stalks where the lush pastures should have been. What hay we got was very good quality, but we have had to sell half of our suckled calves this month as we have not got enough fodder to winter them, and can't buy in unless it's organic. The salt marsh stayed green when all the fields were brown and dusty and kept the sheep going, and then we had rain in August and a very good autumn.

Knowing the car would not pass its MOT this October, we bought a Volvo estate which crossed our path at the right price, but rather a high mileage, and gave the Renault, which had more than 150,000 miles on it, to Barnaby. He drove it all over the country with only the exhaust falling off, and he found it very useful to transport is many belongings every time he moved digs. On its very last weekend he drove seven hundred miles. We have to remember that though its heart was great, its body was a heap of rust.

Natasha continues her turbulent life, but is in touch again and taking two A levels in Bristol. She can't get a grant as she opted out before, so is working during the day to support herself. She discovered her 'other' mother and was most warmly welcomed by her and the rest of the family, but after a while, things seemed to go wrong and she is out of touch with them again. Her many boyfriends are of all ages, types, colours and careers—or otherwise, and some would make your hair stand on end (and I don't mean with little innocent things like earrings and weird haircuts either!).

Barnaby spent last Christmas in Thailand with a friend from

the Foreign Office and survived visits to beauty spots, drug centres, cultural and historical places and erotic dives, which he told us all about in order to watch our eyes popping out on stalks.

He accompanied my father to Canada this year where they canoed up some remote lake together—my father is seventy-five—zipped up the highest building in the world, cable-carred in the Rockies, etc.

Bryony has been to Corsica and Egypt, Matthew to America and France. I need hardly say that we are totally unable to aid any of them financially and what they do is all by their own initiative. My ambition used to be to take them to America, but they have now all been, with the exception of Natasha. Richard's children are the same, only more so as they are nearly all bilingual, and Sophie works in Paris.

We saw Brian recently, just after he had given in his notice to the *Western Daily Press*, or was it the *Bristol Evening Post*? Anyway, he has got his MPhil and has now got a fellowship for three months at Cambridge where he hopes to get his PhD eventually. I am very impressed, as I know I have not got the self discipline necessary for prolonged study.

This typewriter is Bryony's. She borrowed mine for a job application and I now see why. She applied for a job at the National Trust office in Ambleside as assistant to the regional public affairs manager or some such title.

I was very keen for her to get it, we love the Lake District so much I'd like to pass on this passion to one of the children. She came second in their choice, and was rather pleased she had done so well out of one hundred and sixty applicants.

So, not mentioning the mud, dung and worry that makes up quite a lot of the magic on this 'ere marvellous little farm, I wish you a most happy and wonderful Christmas, with love from us both.

Free range hens

Bank House Farm

December 1990

Dear ——

A year of fame if not fortune, of much felicity and even more fatigue. No days the same, nor minutes either. One moment dirty, disgusting or distressing, the next amusing, moving or divine.

Last Christmas we suffered our first serious sheep worrying. To find two young sheep from our replacement breeding flock had been attacked—one dead, one mauled—roused feelings of such anger that I know I would have killed the dog with my own hands if I had caught it. One sheep was dead with its jaw hanging off and another was severely bitten around the mouth (although that one did recover).

Little old Sirius 'popped her clogs' not long after. I howled aloud for the rest of that day and we decided not to have another house dog. However, much worse was the news that Richard's brother in New Zealand had leukaemia.

Robert was forty-three with a little boy of three, and he and Lindy had stayed with us the previous August while on a world trip. By February we knew that he had not responded to the chemotherapy and was dying. At very short notice, Richard and his sister, Hazel, decided to go out there. I had a crash course in the dark on muck spreading (which lever to pull when) and saw Richard off at Silverdale station on a bleak and windy morning. The next three weeks were truly awful, for all kinds of reasons. I think I came quite close to a breakdown (I hasten to add that I did encourage Richard to go). The weather was atrocious, screaming gales and crashing rain every day but two, and naturally I got more and more tired.

One day, when trying to feed a heavy bag of sheep nuts to the ewes, I fell under their onslaught. As I went down, I thought, 'What an ignominious end, being trampled to death by sheep!'

I also felt utterly despicable being jealous of Richard on the golden beaches in the hot sunshine, but I was.

Robert died a week after Richard arrived in New Zealand, and Richard and I met once again on Silverdale Station on a bleak and windy evening, each having had a soul-searing experience, though rather different. Happily, our reunion was as healing and ecstatic as could be desired, and then we were all ready to go into lambing!

But just before lambing, we were on the *On Your Farm* programme. We really did have breakfast, though only Richard managed to eat anything. Claire and Sue were exceptionally nice young women, and did a brilliant job of editing. I enjoyed their visit, but not the actual broadcast and could hardly bear to listen when it was broadcast the following week. Since then we have been interviewed on the local radio, had articles written about us in the local paper, and featured in a glossy brochure produced by the supermarket which buys our meat. We thought a large hamper might be forthcoming from that after I spent a broiling afternoon with dog and sheep until we were all wilting together in front of the camera, but no such luck!'

I have also given a talk on organic farming to the Lancashire College of Agriculture, and the local group of the Friends of the Earth as well as showing interested parties round the farm. My confidence, which was nil to start with, is growing, especially as we believe more and more in what we are doing, and look with greater and greater horror at conventional methods of farming, and what they are doing to the animals and the environment. The National Trust is still keeping an interested eye on us, and brought the chairman to see us recently.

He even had the permanent secretary for the Ministry of Agriculture here, but the government have had other things on their minds lately, and are not doing anything to help.

We were so fortunate not to have the drought, and made a bumper crop of beautiful hay, so the barns are full this year.

Ann and Jack took over for nine days in June, bringing their dogs and goats with them, and coping wonderfully while we went to the Island of Eigg, near Skye.

I *really* needed a holiday by then. We dared to book a cottage this year and luxuriated in hot baths and a real bed. No transport is allowed on Eigg except the resident's Land Rovers, which when parked have to face downhill in case they don't start. The cottage had no electricity, just gas lamps and heaters and candles.

There was no path to the door, sheep cropped turf surrounded it, and the only sounds the sighing of the wind and the singing of the sea.

Coming at last to the conclusion that the dog Dan will be forever dim, (he *still* doesn't know his right from his left) we bought a new collie puppy as Moss is now middle-aged. Silver came from a well-known breeder, trainer and competitor, Viv Billingham. I wanted a long-haired, neat-eared traditional type dog—like Black Bob for those of you who read *The Dandy*—but seem to have got a smooth-haired, prick-eared, funny-faced, mongrel-looking bitch, but never mind, she's working the hens with gusto, aged eleven weeks. She's also turning the house upside down. Very hyperactive. Surely this is a sign of intelligence, or what are we putting up with it for?

Bryony is working in the Head Office of the Shropshire Star and still trying to leave Shropshire for the City Lights—can't think why. Matthew has done a flit from Strathclyde to Bournemouth, but is still friends with Fran, who remains in Glasgow. Barnaby missed a 2:1 by two marks to his disappointment, but my relief that he passed at all. He is working in London for the Universities Athletics Union at £10,500 a year, and busy paying off his student overdraft. His nose has been bashed so many times playing rugby that it now resembles Crinkle Crags rather than the straight edge ruler I used to know and love.

Natasha went to live with an unpleasant man who tried to put her on the streets for his benefit. When he threatened to smash us up if she left him, we retaliated by saying that if he came near here we'd castrate him, having the necessary implements all ready to hand (farming does seem to release the violent instincts in one, does it not?). Since her escape from him she has been in a car crash where her legs were trapped and two people went through the windscreen. (She was in a minicab.) When she was freed, not even her stockings were laddered.

Brian is working in Romania, advising on the setting up of a 'proper' newspaper. None of the people he is working with has any newspaper experience at all, so there are difficulties. Food and hotels are grim, and it's very cold, but it is obviously very worthwhile.

We are expecting to see most of the children over Christmas, except William who is teaching English in a Chinese university for a year. We could do with a few more bedrooms, now that they usually bring partners and prefer more privacy than formerly.

Windy Ridge is still putting the whisky in our glass and proving so popular it's difficult to get in there to do any maintenance and decorating. The poll tax hit us hard and we have had to increase the price rather dramatically and with much trepidation, but so far it still seems to be booking up next year. I really love going up to the Lakes each week, and Windy Ridge is the only place I manage to keep clean and tidy and just about under control.

Concluding this letter, I would say that we are fortunate in getting a lot of appreciation from people and a great deal of pleasure from the animals themselves, but it *is* bloody hard work!'

Happy Christmas and love from us both.

The living room at Bank House Farm

Bank House Farm

December 1991

Dear ——

This time last year I was beginning the countdown to Christmas, more of a military operation than a mere family gathering. Richard's daughter and son-in-law had heard that we have quiet, civilised sort of Christmases and had booked in early. They arrived to find that all my children, plus some partners, were coming, as well as our parents and my sister and other family for Boxing Day. I began making lists and menus and putting food in the freezer weeks in advance, and despite everyone laughing at me for my efficiency, it paid off and we enjoyed a really splendid Christmas, and what's more, I never washed up once.

It went on for days, and I reckoned up that I cooked 197 main meals over the period. William, in China, could not come, and Sophie came for the New Year, which for her was unfortunate as by that time, all money and energy spent, the only way we could face the New Year was in bed watching Clive James (our TV being in the bedroom). Spending New Year's Eve in bed with ageing parents watching TV cannot be a young person's idea of fun.

Soon after this we had a severe frost which burst a pipe at Windy Ridge, which I discovered on a Friday when going to make the house ready for visitors coming on the Sunday. The ceiling paper hung down in wrinkled strips to the carpets which squelched like Lakeland bogs. The pictures on the walls slumped soggy in their frames. Then followed two days of Anneka Rice-like challenge (Richard loves watching Anneka Rice, his *only* concession to pop TV). Despite there being no carpets on the floor, and a somewhat Spartan atmosphere, the visitors would not be put off and during the next fortnight had roaring fires and dried the place out thoroughly. After which I moved in to redecorate, and with the insurance we had beautiful new carpets.

As Ann, my sister, had volunteered to take over the farm again this summer, we thought a holiday at Windy Ridge would enable us to get in some long-neglected walking in the Lakes. Optimistically, we planned to do a few maintenance jobs as well, like re-fencing the boundary and building a new woodshed, and possibly painting the outside—in a week! It proved to be nearly as hard work as the farm. It rained every day, wild, cold, gusty weather, and doggedly we demolished the old shed and built a new one, reminiscent of a stockade in a Wild West film, and strong enough to corral a horse in. We had one good day's walking (in the pouring rain) and then Richard and his cousin Mike sloshed about in the mud and got the boundary fencing done, while I was allowed a day off to visit a friend who had just come out of hospital. It was lovely not having to think about hens and sheep for a week, but otherwise not a success and definitely not a rest.

I got rather paranoid about holidays this year. The lack of them is beginning to tell. I found myself feverishly totting up everyone else's days off, e.g. fifty-two weekends = 104 days = *three months* of each year even *without* holidays, in comparison with us, which equals no weekends at all, and in the last five years, six weeks altogether away from the farm, and *very* lucky to have had that.

Richard bears this with greater equanimity than I do, but even he got to a pretty low ebb by the end of haymaking when we felt like two overstretched bits of worn out elastic.

Last year we finished making a wonderful crop of hay by the beginning of August. This year we couldn't begin until August. To mow or not to mow, to turn or not to turn, to bale or not to bale, that was the daily question, and we agonised over every bale, and in the end were forced to get most of it in too green so that it heated up and lost feeding value. The local contractor made one field into silage which prevented us losing it altogether, and his gigantic machines went roaring and churning round our little fields until it was quite dark, flattening a great swathe of uncut hay across one field in the process.

One of the calves was born unable to excrete and when it died we replaced it with a bought in calf so as not to waste the milk (and that year's profit).

For six weeks we struggled daily with the cow in the hope that it would take to the calf, trying everything that we and everyone else could think of. I hate giving up, but in the end we sent the calf to market and dried off the cow. What a waste.

Meanwhile, among our many visitors, was Richard's little nephew from New Zealand, aged five, who stayed for a week with his mother. (Richard's brother died last year.) His enthusiasm for life, and ability to demand instant and constant attention were about equal. One of our cats, noted for its placidity in a room full of twenty playgroup children, actually jumped clean out of the bedroom window when it heard him coming. Getting him to lower his voice and 'be gentle with the animals' meant that he learnt how to pick up the hens, and I then caught him dunking one in the water trough.

We will pass on to the next visit, when Natasha suddenly arrived with a six-year old Jamaican boy (her lovers' child). Though strongly disapproving of her lifestyle and most of her friends—at one time she was going out with a professional gambler, very rich, whose son was older than she. But we were utterly charmed by Craig, who had been rejected by his unmarried mother, and whose lifestyle we would describe as deprived. And seeing Natasha, to whom I would not have entrusted a guinea pig in the past, actually potting him before she went to bed, and reading him Little Grey Rabbit stories, and handling him like a mother of many, was quite a revelation, amusing and warming. The fact that every night as we were going to bed, she and her friend Liz (a nice girl) took off to the night spots in Morecambe (we didn't know there were any before she came) getting home at 3 am and sleeping until 11 am, made no difference to Craig. He slept until 11 am too and was obviously quite used to fitting himself in with whatever adults he was with. I have not heard since what the situation is, and have no idea what has happened to Craig. He was a dear little boy.

Returning to the farm, which is doing pretty well considering the general farming climate, we have been the subject of a series of articles in *Cumbria Life* magazine (though we are not in Cumbria). The author and photographer Vivian Russell (ex-wife of Ken Russell) has now become a real friend and we have seen a lot of her. She lives in Borrowdale, but thinks nothing of the journey down here and in fact drives to France to her vineyard more often than I get to Kendal. She is very enthusiastic about the farm and hopes to get a book published about it. It is all very easy for us as we don't have to pose, we just get on with whatever jobs we're doing, whether it's taking a farm walk, gutting the hens, lambing a ewe, castrating a lamb, or assisting the boar to serve a sow. Vivian has photos of them all, and they are brilliant.

We have recently applied for the new Land Stewardship Scheme sponsored by the Countryside Commission, which, provided we comply with certain regulations to do with management of the land and conservation of the countryside and public enjoyment, will give us £50 per hectare per year. As we discovered that we are doing all the things already and have not had to change anything, this could mean an extra £1,000 a year to our income, all the more welcome as we may have to keep reducing our sheep numbers as the salt marsh continues to erode and cut down our grazing.

We are sad to be losing our dear Laurence Harwood, agent to the farm and regional director of the North West National Trust, and also Richard's boss. He is moving to a national job with the Trust, although remaining in his home in Grasmere, so we don't as yet know who will take us over. He not only restored our faith in the Trust, but has become a good friend too, so we won't be losing touch.

I refrained from mentioning the menopause in my last years letter, but as it has certainly dominated this year as well, it deserves a few lines, or more realistically, a book. On the assumption that

I, being of sound mind and healthy body (usually) would pass through the menopause without noticing it, it came as a rude shock when it clobbered me like a sandbag. And believe me it's been *grim*. The body, formerly a docile and amenable companion, suddenly passed out of my control like a wayward teenager. I did compose a marvellous and telling poem about it one wakeful night when cooling off after being woken up by molten lava flowing through my veins for the umpteenth time—just one of the symptoms—but could remember nothing of it in the morning. Although deeply suspicious of hormone treatments, I was driven to try HRT twice, but each time activated migraines, which though not bad enough to keep me in bed for long, were not ideal accompaniments to cleaning out the hens or sorting lambs for slaughter.

The health horrors have not stopped there. Recently I caught sarcoptic mange from the pigs. Not something to win you friends or influence people, but a mere minor discomfort compared to the menopause.

To give myself a boost I began a new enterprise, or rather indulgence. I bought a Chinchilla Persian kitten, with the intention of breeding from her. Chrysanthemum is now about five months old, with eyes like a snowy owl and white fur that floats round her like soft feathers. She seems to be turning a rather dirty grey which may be the Chinchilla bit, or perhaps just going under the beds. She also needs combing a lot, but she is a cat of definite character, not at all neurotic, and she eats anything from the cheapest cat food to chocolate biscuits. She had the great good sense and diplomacy to prefer Richard's company to mine when she first arrived.

This year we really are having a quiet Christmas. The children are with Brian who departs to China in the New Year, and my parents are coming here. My mother has suffered severe depression for years which is truly awful for her and my father. All possible drugs have been tried, and electric shock treatment, but to no avail. She's been in ordinary hospitals, nursing homes, and mental hospitals both for her sake and to give my father a break. Though deeply and continually unhappy, she is definitely not mad, and the whole thing is much worse than the menopause! I firmly believe that euthanasia is the answer, not for her because she is terrified of dying, but definitely for me, when the time comes.

To end on a more cheerful subject, we had another brief break in September when we went on a whistle stop tour to see as many children as we could fit in.

Hazel and Michael earned our undying gratitude this time by taking over. Bryony has an exacting but stimulating job on a Portsmouth paper, and now has her eye on Fleet Street in the future. Matthew is computing in Bournemouth and has a car which he finds handy to get him to orienteering venues. Barnaby came down from London—in fact, there were seven of us in a two-bedroomed house, and one of those was occupied by Bryony's lodger. We slept in Bryony's bed and were thankful.

Belinda and Julian have just bought a house and were in the throes of decorating, so it was not easy for them to put us up either. We slept in their bed too, and had to take the washing-up upstairs to the bathroom as the builders were in the kitchen. William came over from Bath, safely home from China. He is planning to go to Japan next to work there for a time. Rather him than me.

This holiday did us a lot of good, especially as we managed to fit in a few visits to friends and relatives, some of whom we hadn't seen for years, and we felt fortified for the winter. I enjoy this time of the year. Almost all the two hundred lambs have been sold, tupping is nearly over and seems to have gone satisfactorily, and all the flock is in one group and on the farm which is easier than looking over four or five groups all over the place. The cows are in, and although they have to be fed twice a day and mucked out every other day, I don't mind that. The piglets won't be ready for pork until January, when we will be busy as there are twenty of them to sell off the farm. The sows are in pig and don't need much attention, not even mucking out as they are free range. We do have

to bump off a house of hens later this week, which is two days'
hard work, but most evenings now we try to finish everything
outside, even grading the eggs, by six o'clock, and then after supper
(and possibly a short doze) we catch up on all the paper work that
has piled up in corners since before lambing, or we read, or even
sometimes go to bed early and watch television.

We hope you'll have a very Happy Christmas.

Much love from us both.

The back of Bank House Farm

Bank House Farm

November 1992

Dear ——

I'm writing rather early this year in order to combine our Christmas greetings with a change of address. For, yes, we are indeed leaving our marvellous little farm and returning to the Lake District. It has been the most extraordinary year. Read on.

I mentioned in my last letter that I had caught sarcoptic mange from the pigs and very shortly afterwards I was rushed into hospital in the dead of night (just like in *Casualty*) with severe chest pains with what turned out to be pericarditis (inflammation of the membranes of the heart). At the time nobody knew what it was and the mention of the mange mites got everybody rather excited and I had visits from specialists in zoonosis or diseases transferable from animals to man.

I noticed that all the nurses wore rubber gloves and thought that this must be a result of AIDS precautions until I realised that it was because of me.

As I haven't been in hospital more than one night in my life I found it all very interesting and stimulating, and as I didn't feel ill, I thoroughly enjoyed the rest and the fuss. It was rather appalling being told to take things easy for three months (what, on a farm!) So Christmas was not very quiet as all the children came up to see me and we had a jolly time and Richard had plenty of help with the chores.

At that moment Britannia the sow chose to farrow and gave birth to one live piglet and several dead ones and then upped and died herself, leaving us with orphan Boris. Have you ever snuggled up in bed with a piglet? He sucked his bottle just like a baby, and went outside to pee. He sat in front of the fire with the cats wearing his little woolly jacket. Unfortunately for him he grew and grew and eventually had to be banished from the house, although he followed us all round the farm causing great amusement. When his charming childish ways changed to belligerent teenage bullyings, he went the way of all poor pigs.

Sometime in February, Richard and I fell into the dumps together and went through one of those bad patches that most marriages experience at some time or other. Exhaustion was the main cause and there didn't seem any way we could combat that. Richard had borne the brunt of my illness; and to spare him, I was really doing too much. The family rallied, in practical terms and also financially, so that we could get some help. Richard flew to the south of France for four days to Vivian's vineyard, which gave him a break. Things being all right again between us, we were into the first week of lambing when I went down with a nasty appendicitis. That really *was* a crisis. I did remember to tell the anaesthetist on my way to the theatre that I was a member of the Voluntary Euthanasia Society and that my donor card was in my handbag. I was deeply impressed by my stays in hospital and thought the staff were wonderful. Again, it was bliss just resting with no responsibilities, and again I was home in three days and told to rest for another three months. Poor Richard!

This time we were fortunate to have a friend, Peter, who needed a base at that particular moment and he was marvellous, and he and Richard coped magnificently and just came to me for advice and instructions. Usually I am in charge of lambing and I found it terribly hard to sit in bed and watch them going out first thing in the morning to do all the things I would normally be doing. Natasha, being temporarily out of work, came to stay (and was brilliant!) and it was decided that I should have a holiday to recuperate and so I found myself on a plane to the vineyard to stay with Vivian and her children which was absolutely wonderful. As well as being a holiday, it restored me to myself. It's a long time since I did anything independently of Richard and I had lost confidence, which is not good.

In May our very dear old friend in Grasmere died, and we were told that she had left us her house and all its contents, the cottage, and the land, and by so doing, changed the direction of our lives once more.

I could write pages about Brenda, she was a very remarkable person and we were very close to her, tears come to my eyes even now as I write, and from the very first time we met her we 'hit it off'. We could and did spend hours talking to her. She lived alone in her big house for twenty-six years, with no help, and only got Richard in to mow her lawns when she was seventy-eight! She was eighty-six when she died and I am sad that she had to die in hospital in the end, instead of at The Wyke which she loved so much. We buried her ashes under her favourite tree, as requested.

Although Brenda left no conditions in her will, we knew that she wanted us to live at The Wyke and if possible to keep it as a whole. It is the most glorious place, overlooking the lake and on the quiet side of Grasmere. The house is large and rambling and in need of total redecoration—we have just had it rewired and re-plumbed—there is a cottage which we will let like Windy Ridge, and about eight acres of grazing land and sixty acres of wild land, only accessible by foot and full of magic secret places where the red deer hide.

We had to give a years notice to the NT and desperately wanted to hand over our animals lock, stock and barrel, so that they did not have to be split up. This has finally been achieved, but not without considerable worry. The new tenant, whom we like, arrives on 28 November (we haven't had to wait a year); we have had a long period of not knowing what was going to happen. To compound this year of ill health, I was then struck down with shingles, which I think was worse than everything else put together. Thank goodness it's now receding, just in time for me to start packing.

We did have some help in the summer. One schoolgirl at Easter doing work experience who was quite good, and then there was Frank. About the only good things about Frank was that he didn't smoke and he didn't smell. I answered an advert for a German Swiss student with experience who just wanted his keep. His actual experience was helping his uncle haymaking for one day when he was six. He hated getting his hands dirty. He hated touching the animals. He thought most things were 'deesgusting'. He brought a huge guitar with him which he played mournfully and tunelessly in the evenings. We tried to persuade him to visit all our children and see more of England, but he wouldn't leave us. Anything that annoyed him he wanted to kill and I really *was* furious when I saw him kicking one of the sheep. We reckoned he would have been an ideal candidate for Hitler's Youth army. What bliss it was when he departed.

We tried to have a family gathering at The Wyke, but that did not come off so we went to Northumberland for a few days and visited all the NT properties for free, which was good, but the best part of that brief holiday was coming back to spend our first night together at The Wyke.

I intend to enter my artistic phase. If I tell enough people I shall *have* to get down and *do* it. We're taking a cow and her calves with us, and a few hens, but we really are trying not to be too tied so that we can go away and visit our children and friends—glorious freedom. As our solicitor said to us, 'You're asset rich, but income poor,' but we are certain we can manage, having had a wealth of experience in that direction.

As for the children, Bryony has recently won a British Telecom Arts Journalist of the Year award, Matthew may be returning to Glasgow (on his unicycle and juggling his balls), Barnaby is off to Africa and India for several months and is working voluntarily there with his eye on United Nations work one day, and Natasha has spent some of this year working in France and Greece. I've started collecting cuddly toys for when the grandchildren come and visit, but so far none in sight. At least now I should have the time to *be* a good grandma!

We wish you a happy Christmas with love.

The Wyke and cottage

The Wyke
Grasmere
Cumbria

Christmas 1993

Dear ——

Life gallops on. A lot of people assume that we have retired, but although we feel we have in comparison to farming, we still have to earn our living, but it seems in the pleasantest way possible, and almost stress free.

The main aims for the year were to get enough beds sorted out for visitors and then to get the main living areas decorated, i.e. the kitchen, rambling hall, our bedroom and bathroom, and to create some light and space around the house which was rather overgrown with trees and bushes. We are on the shady side of the hill which means almost permafrost in the winter. After that it was vital to get the cottage up and running to bring in some income. This became vacant on 1 March and we painted it inside and out by 1 May. I polished the last brass ten minutes before the first visitors arrived. Happily, people love it and are already booking for 1994 and even 1995. Fortunately for us, the time the drains blocked up we had family staying there, and Richard was able to dig up half the garden at his leisure. Fired with enthusiasm, or something, he then went on to sort out the drainage system here, once expertly put down by the Victorians, but untouched (and unused) for many years. No wonder the garden was boggy in places.

We then tackled the outside paintwork, and on all fine days could be seen up ladders or on knees, scraping, sanding, or painting throughout the summer.

I suppose we've done two-thirds of the house, as well as some necessary maintenance at Windy Ridge. The winter project is to get the flat decorated so that we can bring in some more income if needed. There are still a few drawers and cupboards I have not explored yet, but gradually, very gradually, I am sorting and clearing, cleaning and tidying, and I must say, loving every minute.

We have plans for the garden, which is why Richard is putting up a deer fence this winter, because the red deer come and eat off almost everything not protected by wire cages. He spends a great deal of time supplying the cottage, Windy Ridge, and the house with logs. There is an abundance of wood, but all of it is on a slope down or up and generally inaccessible even by wheelbarrow, so it is very hard work getting it.

I have done very little hard physical work this year because the 'shingles' turned out to be the effects of organophosphorus poisoning, which we used to dip the sheep in before we went organic. At its worst I was taking morphine, and am now left with a damaged leg, which is a permanent nuisance. At one time I could not walk as far as the gate as my feet became so sensitive they felt as if they were covered in blisters. Organophosphorus was developed as a nerve gas during the war, and now we dip sheep in it and spray vegetables and grain with it because it is so effective at killing insects. It is poured on to the backs of sheep and cows to rid them of internal parasites and it has still not been banned. It is used in flea powder and sprays too, and is very easily absorbed into the body. The Ministry of Agriculture suggest that the toxic sheep dip should be diluted and spread on the land!

In April I was sent to Preston Royal Hospital for tests including a lumbar puncture. I arrived to find a full scale fire alarm which was unnerving. Nobody knew anything about a bed for me, but once in bed, I discovered that the woman opposite had been sexually assaulted by a male patient while going to the loo. I wondered why the police had seemed more numerous than the nurses. Finally, she went home and the offender stayed! Just round the corner of the open ward was a chap who was escorted at all times by two burly guards. We had plenty of opportunity to goggle surreptitiously at him because the strange system was that all male patients had to go past the women's ward to go to the loo and vice versa. As the results of these tests were lost twice, we were not too impressed with Preston Hospital.

I decided to join a water colour class this autumn, not having done anything in colour for—wait for it—fifty-four years! No sooner had I started to get to grips with that—with great enthusiasm—than I was asked to illustrate a book for a friend. This was to do eighty-four drawings and forty-two maps for a book on walks in Orkney, all in three months. Advance payment nil, but 4 per cent royalties. I can't be doing it for financial rewards, but I am enjoying doing it, even though I didn't even have to go to Orkney.

It has been wonderful not feeling tired all the time, wonderful having time to talk to visitors, and we have had a of visitors, some needing very desperately to talk. For we feel that something is going wrong with the lives of many young people. They seem to be leading immensely stressful lives which don't seem to be leading anywhere, and are certainly not creating happiness or fulfilment, although they are paid such vast sums of money (to us) and they always seem hard up. The ones with jobs are working far too hard and the pressure is so great that if they have a partner they hardly see him/her, and if they haven't, there's no time to find one. Children come nowhere on the list of priorities.

Bryony, now thirty-two, has had a terrible year, combining falling in love, which did not work out after months of agony, with getting the job she wanted—women's editor on the Portsmouth paper—and finding out she was doing the work that three people did before. She was runner up for another award this year, but that has not helped much. She can't sell her house in Shropshire and has to have lodgers there and in her rented house in Portsmouth to pay the mortgage on one and the rent on the other. I went down to help her move house recently while she carried on working.

Belinda's job was so bad in the end that she gave it up after travelling daily to London from Bradford-on-Avon for five years. Her husband was made redundant from his job this year, but they have both got new jobs, Belinda in Cheltenham; and Julian in Trowbridge, working from 2 pm to 2 am. No wonder they all come up here looking pale, thin and shattered.

Matthew, thirty, and Fran split up after seven years. I'm sure that was painful too, but Matthew was never one to bare his heart to anything but a computer. He has been cheered up by getting a job with a big company in Southampton, so surely there will be some super girl there among the one thousand employees.

Barnaby, twenty-four, is back to being a penniless student again, doing an MA in Birmingham, after his travels in India. His work there has made him very indignant about commercial development and exploitation, so he is doing a course on development management, and this time round, is forgoing the beer and the rugby in order to work. He has a really sweet girl (from Bolivia, who addresses me charmingly as Mrs Rosemary) and she is at Sunderland doing maths and engineering.

William is teaching English for another year in Japan and his delightful American girlfriend is an artist. I felt most hopelessly out-of-date when she asked me what my thoughts on art were. I prefer to keep my extremely fuzzy thoughts on art to myself.

Sophie is still in Paris and is fed up with selling Barbie dolls and EuroDisney, although when she described the technology apparently necessary to do this we were all agape with astonishment.

Nicola and her partner are whizz kids in High Wickham, and bomb with aplomb up and down the M25. Richard and I ventured on to it on our brief but extremely enjoyable visit to Kent, surprisingly unchanged, in the autumn. Would that we could create a Sissinghurst here.

Visiting Natasha in London was an experience. After three days of being wined, dined, taken in taxis to theatres and exhibitions and generally spoiled rotten, I felt it would be definitely indiscreet to ask where the money was coming from! She wore the most stunning clothes (even I could tell they were not from M&S) and as she walked down the street men's heads did honestly swivel on their necks.

But, as I arrived, she explained that her flatmate had gone into hiding as her former boyfriend had threatened to 'rearrange' her face and worse, so Natasha was worried that he might appear in the flat which made her (and me) understandably nervous! She has spent five months of the year abroad in visits to places from Venice to New York, but on a more mundane trip to Grasmere recently, she says she is thinking of going to college as 'money isn't everything.' Hurray!

One of the best memories of this year is of taking our little boat out on to the lake early on a summer morning, the two dogs perched up in the bows, and rowing slowly round the island, where there is a heronry, while the morning mist lifts off the surface, revealing the surrounding mountains, and all is calm and beautiful. Come and try it.

We wish you a happy and peaceful Christmas, with love.

The Wyke

The Wyke

Christmas 1994

Dear ——

What to put in and what to leave out. It becomes more difficult every year to be indiscreet (honest) as the people I write about now ask to see what I have written! And, of course, I don't wish to hurt any feelings.

We are still decorating. Only six rooms and a corridor to go and then we shall have completed the whole house and cottage, inside and out. Then there could be a ceremonial burning of the paint spattered overalls—but, hang on, won't the cottage and Windy Ridge still need some ongoing maintenance for years to come? At this moment we are decorating the big room at Windy Ridge, the only chance to get in there, we hope, before Christmas 1995. Bookings are buoyant with the cottage a length ahead at present. Some discerning people prefer Windy Ridge (several have now tried both), including Richard. I think they are both so different it is difficult to compare.

The hit of 1994 has been the red squirrels which have come to both places every day to delight the visitors by raiding the bird feeders which I have had to keep going all year. Costly on nuts, but worth helping the squirrels to survive up here.

An incentive to keep decorating was a neighbours' wedding, in fact, it has been a year of weddings and funerals (we saw the film *twice*) and when we were asked if we did bed and breakfast, naturally we said we did. That spurred us on to make the main guest rooms habitable, plus the dining/sitting room. Richard became the front man, chatting up the guests and getting orders while I frizzled with the bacon and eggs in the kitchen. The flat was completed by the spring, initially for the family to use, but after my father had tried it for a week and decided he would rather stay in his own house, it seemed silly not to put it to good use, which is to help pay the heating bills. That meant creating a garden and laying a path to the door and hauling about a thousand bucketfuls of gravel up the steps.

This is a particularly good house for visitors as we have our own little eyrie complete with bathroom and everyone can get away to peace and quiet should they wish. While waiting for the ever-churning washing machine to disembowel itself, I totted up the number of visitors we have had since January: one hundred and seventy-five visitors who we've accommodated, breakfasted and given an evening meal to—not including the paying ones. We have enjoyed many good evenings over a bottle of wine, and some good days out too, and certainly feel in touch with the outside world and all the stresses and strains therein.

Our own holiday was cancelled because my mother died two days before we were due to go to Switzerland. As it was, both my sister and I were able to be present when she died, in hospital, and were glad that all her fears were groundless and it was indeed a peaceful ending. Her funeral was a simple humanitarian service. I think the main emotions the family felt were a deep thankfulness that her sufferings were ended at last. The other funeral this year was of an elderly farmer who was very kind and helpful to us when we were buying our flock of sheep for the farm. He continued to keep an eye on us and kept in touch. He was buried near his farm in the hills and the service was conducted in a small chapel. So many people came that most of us had to stand outside while the service was relayed to us. Singing 'The Lord is my Shepherd' in the open air, with the sun on our backs and the sheep that he had cared for so well all around in the fields was a truly moving experience.

As for the wedding, well, that was amazing. Richard's second daughter, Sophie, has lived and worked an France for five years and has now married a Frenchman, Marc, an extrovert with a huge smile (and they want children!) We flew to Paris for a fling and to meet him in April for four days. We stayed in their flat on the top floor of an old apartment block near the opera house—why do I always think of the fire risk when further than a few feet off the ground? The wedding was at Freshford, near Bath, where Penny lives. The house and garden is probably bigger than here and made a lovely setting. They had a marquee and Penny and her friend Barbara did *all* the catering for *all* the guests over several days, including the wedding dinner for 130!

It was a stupendous and successful effort and such fun. After the wedding, we went on a nostalgic and extremely enjoyable visit to Dorset and Devon for a few days, which was simply not long enough to see all the people we would have liked to. We renewed our acquaintance with Lord Shelburne, and saw Pinhills again and drove through Bowood to the new golf course where I used to milk cows. All the barns, milking parlour, calving boxes, bull paddocks, slurry lagoons—gone. I felt like Rip Van Winkle, asleep for a thousand years.

My nephew was married in Wales, another super wedding with a Welsh flavour. He and his bride had decided not to have a honeymoon as they are buying a house, and I thought that was a shame, so we offered them the flat and were delighted when they accepted. The weather was glorious too.

The other big event was my father's eightieth birthday party, which we had here and to which all his eight grandchildren and about fifty friends and relatives came.

My catering extended to putting up a houseful of people and a large birthday cake, which bore a passing resemblance to a fire engine which seemed more appropriate than a whisky bottle (he was in the fire service). For the rest, we know some excellent caterers who provided a feast.

The book *Walks on Orkney* that I was illustrating last year came out at Easter. Quite a thrill, and another ambition satisfied. I am now doing one on Shetland. On the strength of that, and *not* on the money received, we hope to go to Orkney next year. The 4 per cent royalties promised have so far brought in £162 for what I estimate was worth at least £1,500 in terms of time at £10 an hour. I don't suppose the Shetland book will bring in any more, so I may not be able to afford to do another (if asked). I have enjoyed doing it and it makes a change from decorating.

I went to etching classes this autumn, which has solved the present problem for the whole family. Unfortunately, it is something that cannot be pursued at home, a press alone costing nearly £1,000, and it is a very messy business.

It was a pity that the cow was due to calve while Richard was sailing on the Broads with his cousin Mike. It meant they always had to tie up near a phone so he could ring to see how the cow was. As another member of the crew was desperate to keep in touch with his new fiancée, I should think the nerves of the remaining crew got fairly jangled. I had to keep a constant watch on her as we suspected twins again so my week of 'space' existed of dashing down to the field morning, noon and night, and in between as well, and not daring to go further than Ambleside.

She still looked like a stranded flying saucer when he got back and was a week overdue when she calved successfully on the May bank holiday, to an audience of at least fifty people lined up along the wall by the road, probably the most interesting thing they had seen on their walk around the lake. Having twins solved the problem of too much milk, so that I could get on with the decorating.

Because the houses on either side of us were burgled (both second homes) and we started to get rather paranoid, the answer seemed to be another dog. Most people would have chosen a burglar alarm, and now I know why. At the time, we decided it would cost the earth to secure this rambling house. No sooner had we started to make tentative enquiries than we found we possessed an enormous German Shepherd dog (please, *not* Alsatian). Too big to breed from and without a single word of command. Happily, he likes people, though not dogs, but we hope his appearance alone will put the burglars off (but not our friends). We have taken him to dog training classes where he was not quite the worst behaved dog, and slowly he is getting more obedient. It certainly makes Moss and Silver seem like absolute paragons of virtue. He is now used to all the cats, dogs, sheep, cattle and weaner pigs, so we are progressing, and strange to say, we're rather fond of him.

News update on the young people. Bryony, after winning another award in Portsmouth, got herself off the dreadfully stressful paper there and is tons happier in Birmingham as a woman's editor. She moved back into the house she couldn't sell in Whitchurch, and is commuting for three hours a day until she can move into the cottage she has bought in Tamworth. As she has just sold her house, this could be soon.

Matthew decided to quit his job at Skandia Life as a nine-to-five job didn't suit him (no stress, and possibly no girls) and he has set up his own business (brave!) in Glasgow, but not with Fran.

Natasha is selling encyclopaedias in London and is good at it. We have seen more of her this year. She was going out with a nice lawyer, but I think they are now just very good friends. Barnaby reports that she is an excellent cook.

Barnaby finished his year at Birmingham University and got his Masters degree with a distinction which would enable him to do a PhD if he chose. At the moment he does not choose, and he is trying very hard to utilise all his training and experience to get into an aid organisation and thence to Rwanda or some such place. He is working temporarily with Population Concern in London on the administration side at the moment, and he is extremely hard up. He owes Lloyds Bank £5,000 as his student loan, and he is due to start paying that back within a few months of his course finishing. He looks a bit lean and hungry, but he's never here long enough for me to fatten him up.

He and Gilda split up in the summer, which he found hard, but he has been consoled since by a Thai girl and then an Italian (and got into a bit of a muddle, we think, with an unintentional overlap). Belinda has an incredibly tough job with Eagle Star. Her husband, Julian, was made redundant for the second time in two years and he is now doing a teacher-training course in London, so she is supporting him at the moment.

Sophie, happily married this year, is involved with promoting EuroDisney, also a pretty tough job.

Nicola is living with Dave and both are pretty high-powered in advertising. They are coming up to see us next weekend which we are looking forward to.

William is travelling in America and India for the next year with Diane. They saved up enough money while teaching in Japan to take a year off. Not sure where this will lead and neither are they.

Now for the old people.

Us first. We continue to learn new and ever awful things about organophosphorus compounds, mainly because I am still affected and therefore still interested. Strange and unaccountable rashes appear and white blood cell counts drop, mystifying doctors, but not us, as we are sure they are all connected. Every night in bed my legs feel as if they are going to explode, but prolonged exposure to a bit of freezing night air (plenty of that here) does the trick and we get off to sleep for another hour or so.

Richard is quite marvellous and is still heaving logs about, is beginning stage two in the cookery lessons: How to Read a Recipe Book and make a meal from it, and has recently started an Ironing Course. As he is a bit self-conscious about these things, perhaps I won't show him this letter either.

My father, mostly known as Roy. Earlier this year he had very bad sciatica, followed by cancer of the prostate which meant an operation, followed by all the symptoms of the menopause as various hormones which fed the cancer had been removed. He had the most terrible hot flushes and got lots of sympathy from me. Despite these trials, he continued to care for and cope with my mother, taking her out of the nursing home three or four days a week, and insisting on cooking magnificent meals for us when we visited them. He missed her very much when she died, but was determined not to get downhearted.

One of the things which helped was planning a trip to America. He has been corresponding for some years with J. K. Galbraith and was thrilled to receive an invitation to dine at Harvard where Professor Galbraith was to speak. He has just come back from that experience.

He bought himself a new car, and then began to get involved with the administration of the nursing home where my mother was, as well as taking out some of the patients who had no relatives to visit them. He has got very fond of the owner/matron who is a mere slip of a girl—well thirty-five actually—and he is busy and happy. He looks no more than sixty and appears to be getting younger every day.

I'm catching him up rapidly.

It seems that life begins not at forty, but at eighty!

On this cheerful note, we wish you a very Happy Christmas and a stressless New Year.

With love from us both.

P.S. Yes, I do know about all the spellings and mistakes, but I honestly haven't time to change them. Must get on with the decorating . . .

Stop the press: Barnaby is off to Cambodia in the new year with Concern. He says that is where all the unexploded mines are!

The back of The Wyke

The Wyke

Christmas 1995

Dear —

I'm writing this on a true busman's holiday, (looking after my sister's pony, donkey, hens, cats and dog) while I have some time to myself. For we have had a busy year. I have had more breaks away from home than for years, thanks to all the marvellous and competent people who have taken over, including Richard.

The first was in January, to help Bryony move house. She had managed to sell her house in Whitchurch after three years and had bought a little old cottage with a large garden in Tamworth. Now surrounded by more modern houses, it still retains privacy and charm. She had enough money to have fun improving it and her job on the *Birmingham Evening Mail* was really enjoyable. All seemed set fair . . .

I saw Barnaby off to Cambodia in January, from Windermere station. If I tell you that in working for Concern Worldwide, he is protected by armed guards, he must never be out after dark, never go on public transport, and never step off the road *anywhere* because of mines, you will understand why I was rather worried before he went. He is the administration officer in Phnom Penh, but sometimes goes out to projects, such as rehabilitating refugees into former villages, etc. People breaking the traffic rules sometimes get shot on the spot, and the government is anything but stable.

The summer, when it came, was so glorious that it is hard to remember the long, cold, wet winter when 106 inches of rain fell in one year. On one day the whole valley flooded and all the roads out were cut off. One of the main becks off Helvellyn, which was diverted years ago to feed Thirlmere Reservoir, broke its banks and the water came churning down the mountain, straight through the village. From our windows on high all we could see was water. What a contrast to the drought later on. For weeks we hovered on the brink of being waterless as all our water comes off the fell. Twice we were saved by a shower, but eventually there was a deathly hush where there is usually a healthy roar. We had to fetch water in cans from the village. A lot of visitors cancelled, so we lost their money. Another stuck it out—but they came from North Yorkshire, so probably going home was no better! We were thankful for our fields by the lake for our cattle and sheep.

Our holiday in Orkney—a wonderful place, colours and light—inspired me to start painting again. It was *amazing* to see the book I illustrated in the shops, and selling. The book on Shetland should have been out this year, but a cock-up in the sales department meant that it never got distributed. So nil payment there.

Richard had a good week on the Norfolk Broads again—men only. We combined a visit to Nicola and Dave's Edwardian house in Teddington with my nephew's wedding in Farnham. A very happy wedding, although the organist forgot to come.

We helped to organise and run the Annual Cumbria Art Exhibition for ten days over Easter. I put five pictures in and didn't sell any. There is no accounting for why people buy pictures and certainly no predictability. It is very interesting watching people buying. This autumn I have been going to pastel classes and really love the medium.

More quick trips down to Bryony, some with Richard to shift sheds, summer house and sofa, and some also for moral support, for Bryony has multiple sclerosis. This news knocked us all back. She has suspected it for some time, with numbness in parts of her body, but when her eyes started to blur, she went first to her very unhelpful doctor (who didn't believe her) and then to the excellent eye hospital. As it is such an uncertain disease there is plenty of room for hope that it will be of the less severe kind. She kept working and remained brave and positive and gradually her eyes improved. The man she has loved for three years left his wife and moved in, much to my relief as I could not bear to think of her upset and alone. After three months he decided to give his marriage another go, so he left. The next day Bryony developed double vision, extreme nausea with it, and so could not drive or work. Stress seems to be a major contributory factor in MS and it certainly applies in Bryony's case. Ray returned to Bryony after two weeks and, I hope, for good. I will refrain from saying what I thought and felt at the time, and actually, we do like him.

Natasha had us on the hop in the spring, by ringing up to ask if I minded if she got married in two days' time. I was *delighted*. I sent her my grandmother's ring and thought earnestly about them on the day—only to find that they hadn't got married after all. She had only known Andy three weeks and when we met him we liked him too. Tall, good-looking, intelligent, articulate, and a job lined up as a lawyer when he finished his studies. Things seemed to fall apart after that, although they say they love each other, but can't live together. Since then, Natasha has moved into a little cosy cottage in Kent and acquired a cat, neither of which has stopped her extraordinary lifestyle, most of which I don't know about, and the rest of which I couldn't possibly divulge. I don't understand anything about the younger generation. Nor about the older generation either, read on.

Matthew has his head well down in his own computer and company, which has not yet sold any of his brainchildren. I dragged him away for two days on the West Highland Line—great scenery and very good company. I am still waiting for him to meet the girl of my dreams.

Belinda and Julian have separated, having drifted apart, and she is doing well at Eagle Star in Cheltenham after the very tough time they gave her last year. Now she has met a black born again Christian and we are meeting him next weekend. Richard's children all came for Easter, which was really great and the first time Sophie and Marc had been to The Wyke since the wedding. Sophie has been rather fed up with her job at EuroDisney, but they have marvellous holidays which compensate.

Nicola and Dave are going out to Argentina for three years with Unilever. Nicola is giving up her marketing job and they will let their house.

William is of a different ilk and has few possessions and no ties. He became a Buddhist, and shaved his hair off initially (not flattering). On his return from travelling in South America he stayed here, *en route* to Samye Ling, a Buddhist centre in Scotland. He was often seen on his head on the back lawn, apparently talking to himself (mouth exercises actually). We did hope he wasn't putting off our visitors in the flat. He was very willing to help Richard build walls, etc., but by the time one and a half hours of vital yoga was completed each morning, the work was either well under way or done. He is now teaching English in China at the university where he taught several years ago, and is really on his way to Japan and India again.

The lettings of the cottage and Windy Ridge have been excellent and the maintenance and improvements of houses and gardens keep us very far from retirement. The flat helps to pay for the aforementioned improvements. I am determined to finish the decorating of the house *this* winter. Only our big sitting room and the back kitchen areas to do, thank goodness.

We have a few free range hens now, and bought three weaner pigs again in the summer. The idea was to let them dig up the bracken in the woods. They ignored the bracken and loved the woods. We were lucky to get a sighting of them once in three days. They would return to their snug shelter and food when it rained. We presumed they ate acorns and fungi for they grew fit and fat and now, I fear, are in the freezer.

Having got everything in a vague sort of control, we are now turning our attention to the long-neglected woods. Richard has applied for a Woodland Grant Scheme, which means maintaining walls, fences, etc., and keeping sheep out so that regeneration takes place. Trees need thinning out, which will provide us with logs.

Many of the walls have fallen down and there are no fences

and the land is steep and inaccessible. The idea evolved (mainly from me) that a pony could, would, should help us carry fencing materials up and logs down. With the aid of the unexpected bonus of the sheep quota we received this year from the farm, we have put up a stable and fodder store, and Rex arrived last week. He belonged to a pony rescue association and we will be inspected regularly. They think he will be up to the job despite being twenty-two years old. He's sturdy and placid and his knees look in better shape than mine.

We tracked down a pack saddle in Warrington and we're introducing him to his new role of pack pony. He didn't think much of it as he tried to take a chunk out of my thigh (fairly successfully too). Still, biting apart, he has been very good so far. Pack ponies have been used for centuries in the Lake District, carrying lead from the mines, wool from the farms and most other necessities. The packhorse tracks can still be traced over the mountains, and we like to feel we are reviving traditions and not moving too quickly into the technological age.

The pony mania seems to be affecting the whole family, for my father, now eighty-one, is just learning to ride. The incentive, we feel sure, is his friend Carol, with whom he is still totally and obsessively besotted. She, now thirty-six, has ponies and hunts in the winter. Forgotten are his prostate cancer, his sciatica, his sorrow. On with the riding hat, the breeches, the boots. We really are glad that he has found life after my mother, and yes, we do like her, but love has not changed him for the better, and he is more like a tiresome teenager than an aged and respected parent. Need I say more?

After the complete family Christmas last year, we will be on our own, except for Christmas Day at my sister's with our father, and, of course, with only the dogs, cats, hens, sheep, cows and Rex to keep us company.

We wish you a very happy and stress-free Christmas,
With love from us both.

Dogs and cats at The Wyke

The Wyke

Christmas 1996

Dear ——

Six o'clock on a cold and frosty morning. Snow on the mountains and stars still glittering in the sky. Across the lake the street lamps of Grasmere twinkle. It's too early to get up to do the animals, especially the pigs who like to lie abed, so it's a good time to write the Christmas letter.

Last Christmas was something of a surprise—we were snowed in! We could not go to my sister's for the day as planned, and our visitors could not get to us—(just my father actually). So we went to the candlelight service on Christmas Eve, followed by carol singing round the village—the hotels are notoriously generous with wine and mince pies—and enjoyed a glorious walk on the snowy, sunny fells on the day. No matter that we did not have a turkey, we have plenty of our own meat in the freezer. And the quiet that descended on the valley with no traffic noise was so marvellous.

After that I prepared for my visit to see Barnaby in Cambodia. As an unintrepid traveller I was nervous, in fact, petrified, but determined to get there, despite leaving Richard for three weeks. It was great to see Barnaby again after a year.

I stayed first in Phnom Penh, in the house he lives in, with its high spiked gates, guards, tiled floors, ceiling fans, food from the French supermarket (cooked by the maids) and the regular power cuts. Outside, the dusty potholed roads, coconut palms, faded elegant houses, and the thronging, industrious Khmers.

Barnaby had the use of one of the Concern vehicles and seemed to have mastered the art of driving in the teeming traffic, where there are no traffic lights, few signals given, no lights on most vehicles and a thousand motorcycles to every car.

If there is an accident, you get out, quick, before the mobs converge and guns get drawn. The motorcycles are the main transport for everything, whole families, market produce, mattresses, live pigs trussed up like sausages. I saw a woman balancing nonchalantly on the back, suckling her contented baby, while her husband drove, holding two young children between his arms. Not a helmet in sight.

I was taken to Barnaby's office (interesting), to some of the projects in the countryside (fascinating), to Angkor Wat (mind-blowing), to some of the Killing Fields (shocking), and to the terrible Tuol Sleng museum (utterly horrifying).

We stayed in another of the Concern houses in Siem Reap (not far from where the mine expert was kidnapped a few weeks later) for the exploration of Angkor Wat.

I took to my bed under the mosquito net early one evening, and was alarmed to hear sounds of distant rioting. However, it didn't get any closer. In the morning, I discovered the lads had been watching a football video; they can't get TV.

The Khmer people appear calm, stoical and caring, particularly to the children—beautiful, charming, slender children, playing safely in the roads, in the markets, in the schools, caring for their younger siblings in a freedom we have totally lost in this country. There were many limbless people, particularly in the country areas. Most people of my age were brutally killed by the Khmer Rouge, so the population is strikingly young, and my grey head was conspicuous for its rarity. Barnaby told me I looked pretty good for sixty. I said, 'I may be looking forward to being sixty, but I'm only fifty-six!'

On the surface, all is well, but I was dogged with a sense of unease. Barnaby is in charge of security information as well as administration, and any incident is reported to him. He was robbed at gunpoint shortly after I returned and security was tightened. Going out to the projects, one travels in convoys and no one is allowed outside the city after dark (6 pm). The Khmer Rouge are still active, still laying mines, and the army is not to be trusted. I don't remember seeing any police, ambulance or emergency vehicles anywhere.

From Cambodia we flew into Laos, staying in Vientiane in a cheap Chinese boarding house (another experience for mother!) and from there to a log cabin guest house, to which we travelled first by local crowded bus, which plunged in and out of the craters in the dirt roads, rocking from side to side, sucking great clouds of red dust through the open windows, and blasting out cheerful music the whole journey. I couldn't help but to compare it with the Langdale bus creeping sedately up the valley with a couple of people sitting gloomily on board.

The bus took us to the boat, a long, narrow, shallow and extremely unstable boat, upon which we perched—even to turn one's head made it wobble—and so upriver to the log cabins, where Barnaby was able to walk in the mine-free woods, and we sipped the local brew from a communal pot by a big log fire in the evening.

Then to Thailand and Bangkok by overnight train (unforgettable) where Barnaby was enthralled by 'real' shops and spent some time going up and down the escalators and tasting 'civilisation'.

I was never so thankful to return safely to good old England (and Richard) and felt I should never complain about anything—government, health service, traffic, weather, food, etc.—again.

At Easter we were involved once again in the local art exhibition, and I sold a picture; and Natasha got married! You may be surprised, but not half as much as we were, when we received her phone call just after the wedding. Her husband is the lively young lawyer Andy, whom she *didn't* marry the year before, and so we had met him and liked him. They are coming for Christmas this year, with his parents, and Bryony and Ray and dog, and Hazel, Richard's sister, and dog, so I hope they all get on, especially the dogs!

Maintenance of the burglar deterrent, alias the German

Shepherd, has been expensive this year. Caspar has accidentally bitten Richard twice, mistaking Richard's arm and hand for the stick he was throwing. He also tripped me up on the stairs, when I broke the bannister rail, but not my shoulder, though it felt like it, and he got an infected foot after his annual spell in kennels. Once in the surgery (after all the other dogs in sight had been evacuated) he was fine lying on his back and waving his foot in the air for anyone to examine. Still, he has kept the burglars at bay.

While he was in kennels, we were in Shetland. We didn't see anyone with 'my' book, possibly because there wasn't anyone there. The whole of the British Isles enjoyed glorious weather that fortnight—except Shetland. Our cottage was grim, dim, and dirty. The interior of the islands is all peat bogs. The extensive coastline would be lovely if the sun shone—when? We saw otters and birds and crumbling ruins and the places I had drawn were recognisable and the walks in the book were very helpful, but even Grasmere, with its heaving mass of tourists seemed preferable to the bleak treeless solitudes of Shetland.

Our other break was to an Organic Farming Conference weekend in Herefordshire's beautiful countryside just before the hop harvest. Very foolishly, we admit, we came home from that with another cow and calf. Well Florence, a tiny Jersey, was in need of a good home and no one else wanted her. She was supposed to be easy to milk and to get in calf and would come when called. As yet we have not been able to cancel our milk delivery, and to get even a pint we had to sing 'God Save Our Gracious Queen' which is the only tune I can summon at will, and besides, has a wonderful milking rhythm to it. In the summer it had its moments—how many people have watched red deer in the fields while milking down by the lake—albeit on their knees in the wet grass, but it is more comfortable sitting on a bale of straw in the barn where she doesn't seem to need the national anthem. We have had great difficulty getting Florence and Buttercup in calf this year, (a local farmer says it's the polluted lake water) but they have at last coordinated to just miss Nicola's wedding next June. For Nicola and Dave are getting married next year. They have been together for five years, their darling baby was born in August and she is being christened at Christmas. It seems a bit topsy turvy to us, but we make no comment. They are living in Argentina for three years, and as Richard's second grandchild will be born and live in France next March, alas, we shan't see much of either.

William is teaching English in Japan and is learning acupuncture (which may well come in useful for his ageing relatives in the Lake District). He has no partner at present, and neither has Belinda, who is still working for Eagle Star Insurance. You may have seen their adverts on TV which she was responsible for and have done well.

We have had visits from everyone this year which we have really enjoyed.

Matthew has just brought his girlfriend Jenny to stay and we hope it will be a long-term relationship. She got him to buy some proper walking boots and got him up the mountain, and is definitely lifting his nose from the grindstone where it has been stuck since he started his own business. This has not got going yet (financially), but he is still confident. Her father was a nuclear physicist at Sellafield, so our conversation was a little cautious at times.

Bryony and Ray and his two teenage children came for a week, and Amanda was thrilled to ride, wash, groom and muck out the pony. As self-confessed townies, they headed for Blackpool one day, but we did get them up in the woods for a barbecue with Rex carrying the food and gear up in his panniers, and they had a morning messing about in the boat. Nice kids who seem to be coping with all the changes in their life. Bryony had a long spell with her MS fairly inactive, but at the moment her lower half is numb, although she continues to work, drive, and lead a normal life. She came up here in October to lend moral support when I went to Penrith auction to buy a Fell pony colt foal. I thought Hereward the Wyke (what else?) would come in useful when Rex has conked out—if we have not. The log transporting by pony was quite successful, though very hard work for us all. So we are getting him used to being led, tied up, etc. as he is still only a baby.

Our Woodland Grant Scheme is going ahead. The grants come in, walls go up, trees come down, and fences skirt the woods. We are applying for permission to rear and release barn owls here, and for this our habits and habitats come under close scrutiny. The Department of Environment has its claw in this.

My father—he of the mad, passionate and mainly unrequited love for a woman of his granddaughter's age, has this year caused a family rift. We admired him when he took up riding aged eighty-one, we encouraged him when he took up writing his memoirs. He has called it *As I Saw It* and there are no holds barred. This did not matter until he decided it was good enough to publish. The chapter on his family, and particularly on his sons-in-law, is so inaccurate, scurrilous, and grossly insulting that the Grand Canyon is not deeper or wider than the rift between us. I thought I had always been and would be a loving and dutiful daughter, but I now know there are limits. We all think he is deluded about many things—but try telling *him* that. He has said that he is 'not changing a bloody word', so at the moment I can't see a way out.

No wonder there are feuds and wars in the world, and it's coming up to Christmas too, which should be a time of peace, love, reconciliation and good cheer.

We wish you all of these things, and hope you have a wonderful Christmas.

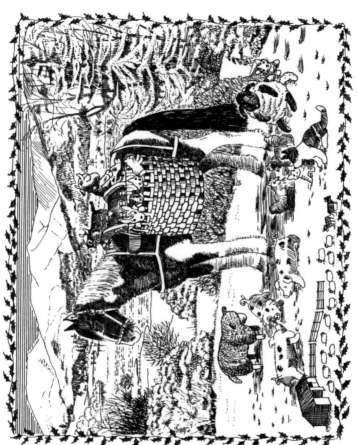

Rex the rescue pony and the rest of our animals as toys

The Wyke

Christmas 1997

Dear ——

Ha! We have moved into the computer age. I vowed I would
be one of the last people to get into the technological world, but
I bought a redundant computer from Matthew as he needed the
money and Barnaby is here to set it up. Yes, Barnaby is back
from Cambodia. He completed his contract recently (mother
breathes sigh of relief) and promptly got a job with Oxfam in
Rwanda (good for him, but not for mother). More of this later.

We had an Agatha Christie house party Christmas last year,
with people who had never met converging on The Wyke from
all over Britain. Happily, no one was murdered and we had a
really fun time, with Bryony's limericks breaking the ice.

In January it was Richard's sixtieth birthday. Despite his
protests we had a party—a great family gathering. Nicola and
baby Isobel came from Argentina to be there. Brenda always said
it should be a family house and this year it has excelled itself.

The local art exhibition involved us again right over
Easter, and we also sold Windy Ridge, lock, stock and barrel.
Friends who had stayed there every year for ten years bought
it and continue to run it as a holiday house, which made it
an easy transfer. It could have been so complicated, with all
the bookings. We did feel sad but it has made life easier (less
washing, gardening, decorating, maintenance), and we have
invested the money—ethically—as we need the equivalent
income in order to stay here.

These changes concentrated our minds on our future here.
We are fortunate to have options, but I think it will be death
or disability that decides us. I had a knee cartilage operation
in April, after months of problems and not knowing what the
problem was. This brought home pretty forcibly that living

here unable to work (as we must to stay here) would not be much fun for either the fit or the feeble.

The flat is now let almost all the year and as we seem to be control freaks we strive to keep it all in order and up together. Having help is not a financial option.

Richard's arduous bracken cutting 'up top' has been so successful that we had the sheep and ponies up there for the summer. It begins to look like fields again. More walls have been built up and we are starting to gate the gaps. We would like to make a contoured track up the very steep bit behind the house. Getting up there would then be easy and pleasant. It was impossible when my knee was bad.

The barn owls came and went. We fed dead chicks to them for weeks until they flew. They may return to breed in the barn but at least we didn't find any bodies. The red deer and roe deer have been down to the fields every night for weeks, eating all the acorns (good) and all the grass (bad) but a magnificent sight. The badgers are active, digging up the fields for grubs but have not been sighted. We haven't seen much of the red squirrels this year but a grey has been seen in Grasmere (bad).

The summer was wonderful, enough rain to prevent worries about no water, and plenty of hot sunshine. Lots of visitors here and some glorious days out.

Florence is now an only cow as Buttercup failed to get in calf, and Lolita and Hiawatha, the heifer and steer, recently went into various freezers, along with the six unplanned lambs whose mothers got out on the fell with a randy ram. I milked Florence all last winter, which must have saved us some money. The pleasures of having a cow's tail wrapped around ones head, smearing ones glasses, have not diminished.

We wisely decided not to have pigs this year due to the number of weddings in the summer, as, believe it or not, we try to keep our lives simple!

My favourite, but highly neurotic, cat died of a tumour, but we had already decided to keep one of Chrysanthemum's kittens so we still have four cats. Due mostly to the programme *Pet Rescue,* to which I am now addicted, we took on a lurcher in September knowing nothing of her past. We discovered that she was a killer of hens (bad) and rabbits (good) and undoubtedly if unsupervised, cats (appalling). OK, OK, it's crazy to have four dogs, but watching the people on *Pet Rescue* makes me feel quite normal, nay, exceptionally sane. Slowly and patiently we make progress. Richard is exceptionally patient with all this. She is a delightful dog and Caspar, the doggy equivalent of Idi Amin, is delighted with her. Moss and Silver accept resignedly whatever new animal appears on the scene.

The big event of the year here was Matthew and Jenny's wedding in early August, which they chose to base at The Wyke, to our great pleasure. Small but beautiful. Not getting married in church caused problems with Jenny's parents, but support from her brother and sisters made it a very, very happy day. Thanks to a legacy from an aunt, I was able to fly Barnaby home for the occasion, although he had to fly back the next day. He had been trapped in Phnom Penh during the shifting of power and the shelling, and communication with him had been impossible, so it was a very anxious time for me and made his return very special. Matthew and Jenny metaphorically pulled up the drawbridge and honeymooned in the flat. Their business has not yet taken off though the future looks brighter. We are all hoping that Jenny's treatment for breast cancer does not make her sterile as she wants children and I may yet be a grandmother!

Bryony's MS has caused problems this year and she has had steroid treatment twice because her legs have been badly affected. Ray has had to work terribly hard all year, and now the Mirror Group have taken over their paper. Redundancies have already started so despondency, low morale and uncertainty are rife. Bryony is still working and is battling bravely. They hope to get married next year and would like to change lifestyles, but when and how?

Natasha and Andy have moved to Malmesbury and have set up their own business as agents to football players. They are also setting up an organisation to help inner city schools provide sports training as a charity (getting professional players involved with the children). I visited them in Kent and helped with the garden. Natasha borrowed a neighbour's lawn mower and cut the lawn in her high heeled boots. As the only tool they had was a bent hand fork we had a good spree at the local garden centre.

Barnaby is going as finance and administration manager for Oxfam in Kigali. I have just discovered that Rwanda is on the equator and I'm already on a learning curve re. Africa. There is a book by Fergal Keane called *Season of Blood* which I'm not sure I should read as I believe it's worse than the book on the Pol Pot regime, *River of Time*, which had my knees knocking before he went to Cambodia.

So we're keeping our fingers crossed for all my children and some of Richards' too.

Sophie and Marc (in Paris) had a baby in February. Although Lily had problems to start with, she is now fine. They came for a long weekend in October. They were exhausted as Mark has hepatitis C and has been on interferon for a year. They are both working full time although Sophie would much rather be home with the baby, but they have big financial commitments (helping to keep Marc's grandfather in a nursing home and a new flat). So we had a lazy time baby-gazing and thoroughly enjoyed it.

Belinda gave up house, job, car, and handbag, and is doing a design management course at Brunei University. She should be writing about her experiences as a present day student as they are very amusing.

William has returned from Japan and is studying acupuncture in York. As it is only every other weekend he is trying to find a job and accommodation to fill the gap. He is still keen on travelling the world, and he remains a Buddhist.

Nicola and Dave and baby Isobel came back to England for

their simply splendid wedding in June. A great party! The vicar fitted the baby into the service with great aplomb.

The third family wedding took place in Cambridgeshire in September, which gave us another super weekend away.

All these weddings disrupted our normal holiday so we decided on a week in the Lake District. Yes, really. We took a cottage in Martindale, unspoilt and remote from all crowds. A wonderful week and a great success, although I did my back in on the second day and could only hobble down the valley floor while Richard strode the tops. I was reminded of a quote from a TV play 'old age is like being punished for a crime you haven't committed.'

You may be wondering how my father is. Very gradually we resumed 'normal service'. The subject of the memoirs being printed was dropped after first a friend and then a granddaughter read them and blew up. His prostrate cancer appears cured, his sciatica has gone, he looks extremely well, younger than ever in fact. He walked five miles round the lakes in the pouring rain with his beloved recently; something he would never have done BC (Before Carol). He sees her once or twice a week and she has him under her thumb, possibly the only person who has managed it, I guess. We like her, but still think he is deluded. He bombs down the motorway at 90 mph, loves his whisky, fries himself a huge supper every night, and, one has to admit, is remarkable for eighty-three.

That seems to conclude this year's news. I now have to get Barnaby to help me print this. One cannot predict the future, but you can be pretty certain I shall not be recounting a trip to Rwanda in my next Christmas letter.

We hope you have a safe and happy Christmas. What else is more important than family and friends in this uncertain world?

The Badger Flat

The Wyke

December 1998

Dear ——

Well, it's happened—I'm a grandmother! Not exactly the uncomplicatedly joyful event one might have hoped for, but glad tidings nevertheless. More of that later. It's been an up and down year, beginning with Barnaby's departure for Rwanda after Christmas, where he is working for Oxfam as their financial administrator. He says the Rwandans are still very traumatised, which is hardly surprising.

I'm not much less so at the thought of him out there. He took his leave in France and followed the World Cup, for which he got five—yes, five—tickets, which was probably Rwanda's entire quota. You may remember that a group of Rwandans were watching the matches when the whole lot got slaughtered (they were in a pub watching the TV).

Just after he had left, a Jack Russell puppy crossed my path, *exactly* like Milly-Molly-Mandy's dog Toby in the books I loved as a child. Sirius was supposed to be like Toby, but turned out rather hairy. So we then had five dogs, which I agree was mad. Completely unfazed by Caspar's huge jaws and paws and Flight's killer instincts, she has given us and them hours of amusement and pleasure. Much later in the year, Moss, our first proper sheepdog and faithful friend, had to be put down, and Flight died after major surgery so we are down to three, *much* more manageable, although we were very sad.

Three really good friends have died this year too. No wonder we've been down.

Shortly after getting Poppy the puppy (my substitute grandchild) Bryony announced that she was producing the real thing, and we were overjoyed. She believed she had the type of MS which progresses slowly and her consultant said to go ahead if she wanted a baby. Unfortunately, she had extreme sickness combined with a nasty attack of MS and was more or less confined to the sofa for months, feeling unbelievably awful. This was a worry! At last she improved and was able to return to work. Her car is now adapted with hand controls and she has a stair lift. For the last few weeks she was able to work from home.

Ray was marvellous throughout, and totally supportive.

During my visits there I kept their garden more or less under control (lovely to dig *real* soil!) but this has not done my knee or back much good. I've recently discovered an excellent osteopath, and we do a bit of Cumberland wrestling together which I find highly embarrassing as I'm half dressed, and he's a lot younger (and slimmer) than I am. I'm still on a list for another cartilage operation.

Last January I became the *Westmorland Gazette* correspondent for Grasmere. No qualifications needed and as anything I did was an improvement on the last correspondent there was no worry, only hassle! Few people come to me with news, so I have to go and get it, so I now know many more people and feel more involved. Almost too much. We're still on the committee of the Cumbria Local Arts, where I sold one picture at the Easter Exhibition, and three more at the exhibition in Ambleside, which does at least pay for the framing. Richard is on the committee of Grasmere Residents Clean Lake Group where they discuss sewage and more sewage, and I am involved with the Grasmere Disability Access Audit where we poke around pavements and premises and look out for obstructions and orange badge bays.

Richard is in the Players' Panto this year. With other unlikely residents, he is doing a sort of Full Monty act, but, no, it's not a complete strip—they get down to long johns and exit to howls of frustration (we hope). I was asked to design some of the set, but thankfully have not had to paint the backcloths.

He continues to go to a music appreciation afternoon where they all hope to get the back seats where they can snooze unseen, and I have begun a batik class in Kendal. Good fun, and it all helps to get us through the winter. We needed something to get us through the summer this year. The rainfall so far is 103.5 inches. Thirty-one inches of that fell in October and November, and three and a half fell on one day. No mud, no flood, just the becks roaring and the lake up a bit. It doesn't seem to have affected bookings and both the cottage and flat are already booking well for next year (thank goodness).

Our holidays took us to Lincolnshire, the Isles of Scilly and finally to Derbyshire where we stayed in Brian and Fran's holiday cottage in order to be within a hour's drive of Bryony, who was booked to have a caesarean birth. Tristan Jamie had other ideas and arrived a fortnight early in double quick time and naturally. It was not Bryony, but the baby who was taken into special care because he was breathing faster than normal. The cause is still unknown despite numerous tests, x-rays and scans. We entered a new world of incredibly tiny babies (though he weighed a respectable six pounds and ten ounces) and babies with all kinds of problems. Bryony persevered with breast feeding throughout all this anxious period. Now he is home, but he is not growing. At twelve weeks of age he weighed just over eight pounds! I am convinced he is not getting enough to eat, but nobody will listen to fuddy duddy grandma! So I worry about that! The health visitor does not believe in mixed feeding, so all my pleas to top him up fall on deaf ears.

I have had experience with hundreds of young animals (and babies) and the whole thing seems extraordinary.

Natasha and Andy decided to move back to London after a year in Malmesbury so that Andy could have a base for his job. They are cheerful, hard-working, but, alas, still smoking. Matthew and Jenny have just come back from a conference in Los Angeles, though still poorer rather than richer. They too work together.

Belinda finished her course in design management near Reading and decided to take off to the Andes for three months on her own. She and Richard spent a day using a compass and a stove up on Silver Howe behind us, which seemed sensible.

Nicola is expecting her second child in March, and Dave is

considering a job in Jakarta with Unilever as he has completed his job in Argentina. We had a lovely visit from them, but two-and-a-half-year-old Isobel treats us as strangers, as does little Lily in Paris. She is one and a half and goes every day to a nursery school, as Sophie is now working full time again. Not good. Sophie doesn't like it either.

William is incommunicado in a Buddhist retreat in the Scottish Borders, which shattered Richard. Not something *he* would, could, or should do. We took William there and it was interesting, but alien with the temple and the stupas looking rather strange in the bare rolling hills and forestry plantations.

His 'mentor' has been on two very severe retreats, each one of forty-nine days in total darkness and alone. Richard was not amused to see William prostrating himself before a golden Buddha. We try to understand. He is there for a year.

As for my father; he is absolutely fine. He went to China on a package tour and returned so enthusiastic about China that he read every book on China that he could find in the library. One of which said that according to various signs, he would die when he was eighty-four. He is eighty-five next August. This has not put him off signing up for a visit to Sri Lanka in February.

Richard's father used to say, 'Everyone over sixty should be encouraged to take risks.' He was a doctor, and we thought this rather amusing, until suddenly we now realise it's *us*. Richard is sixty-one, I am fifty-nine (and Bryony is thirty-seven.) Incredible!

It's been back to the typewriter this Christmas, but twinges of uneasiness are impinging with the realisation that I'm going to be completely passé with the next generation if I don't learn to speak their language. Perhaps next year's course had better be 'getting to grips with your computer' as I seem to have acquired two, both of which lie around like dead dinosaurs and so far have been completely useless.

We do hope you have a really happy Christmas, and a splendid 1999. With love from us both.

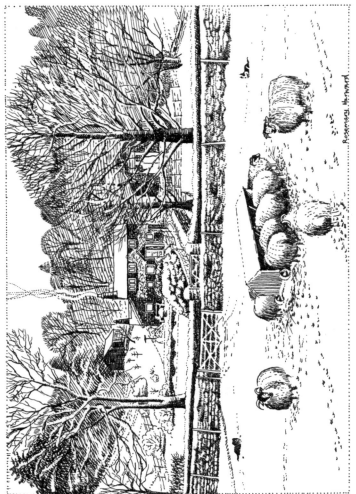

The Wyke cottage and our sheep and dogs

Rosemary Harward

Upper House,
Suckley
Worcester

Christmas 1999

Dear ——

If last year had its ups and downs, this year has been like a roller coaster.

One of the ups was Bryony and Ray's wedding in May which took place from The Wyke. Knowing then that we were leaving made it a very happy and sad occasion. Bryony is the ultimate organiser even from a distance and because of her incredible attention to detail, the day was perfect. Her legs were so bad then that she could walk no further than a few steps for the ceremony in a hotel beside Lake Windermere, but her determination and bravery brought tears to more eyes than mine. Tristan sat solemnly on my knee in his matching outfit (full bridal regalia!) and was unbelievably good throughout the whole long day, which included a boat cruise on the lake and further gatherings back at The Wyke. We had at least fourteen people staying for the whole weekend. After a week in the flat, Bryony and Ray went to Italy for a week and I continued to look after Tristan.

We had made the major, major decision to sell The Wyke in March, both in order to help Bryony practically and financially, and because we could see the inevitability of this in the future, as without help The Wyke would either deteriorate or kill us. It was nonetheless a very agonising time and Richard got clinically depressed and is still on pills.

The plan was for us to move first, choosing somewhere near enough to be of help when they moved to a bungalow, which had to be near enough to Ray's work in Birmingham. Bryony needs flat ,safe pavements and easy access for her wheelchair and electric scooter, and we are still hooked on country living, black skies at night and quiet. Birmingham itself was not an option! It took two brief days to find a house we liked, and that is when the stress began. Because we had not put The Wyke on the market first (well, who would, not knowing where they were going) we were in danger of losing this one for months. There was the added worry of the cottage and flat and all the bookings, and, of course, the animals.

Parting from them, even to good homes, was extremely painful. We are determined to have no more cows, hens, sheep or pigs, and the only way to resist this is to believe that we can have the freedom to go away any time. So we have just bought a small, old caravan!

As we wanted to sell The Wyke as a whole, as we were given it, we were pleased that the new owner took over everything, though he is letting the cottage and flat through an agency, and the land to a local farmer and he employs a gardener-cum-handyman for the gardens and house. He also intends to use his yacht in Majorca when the weather is bad in Grasmere.

For my sixtieth birthday in July we had booked to go to Switzerland (I did not want any more celebrations) and although we thought the country was absolutely wonderful, the holiday was marred by anxieties about the move, and Richard's excessive fears and worries.

The house move was a three-day affair, not helped by a delay in our money coming through, so that when we arrived here at 9 pm the owner would not let us in, nor the lorries next morning. We had three cats and two dogs and Natasha (who had helped us move and was brilliant) in the car. Complete numbness set in and we could hardly believe it when, after much consultation with solicitors, we were allowed to start unpacking, a moment fixed for ever in our minds, as the eclipse began just then.

From the moment we left the Lake District, Richard has been a new man. He loves it here and is entirely happy doing all the many jobs needed (many, many more than we thought). Strangest of all, he has taken to cookery and now elbows me out of the kitchen. He can hardly wait to get to his cookery class 'Man in the Kitchen' at

Malvern College. We discovered that the pills he is on are Prozac, and I recommend them heartily.

Upper House is seventeenth century, and its floors, ceilings and walls slope and tilt at all angles, creating strange optical illusions. It is down a tiny muddy lane and is very quiet and private, with tranquil views of the Malvern Hills in the distance. It is sunny, compact and warm. We have three bedrooms and a study upstairs and have made the dining room into a bedroom for Bryony if she stays. We eat in the large farmhouse kitchen and the builders have just completed a downstairs walk in/wheel in shower room, an upstairs *en suite*, a new boiler and Aga and woodstove.

The sitting room looks out south over a big lawn with trees and shrubs, and there is an acre of paddock, and the buildings were once a cider house and hop kilns. There is a hideous corrugated barn which is useful to store the caravan, the sheep trailer and the wood store.

The countryside is real 'heart of England', extremely rural, rolling hills, woods, rich brown earth and a mixture of cattle, sheep, and crops ranging from wheat, hops, vines and apple orchards. Thick mud on our boots and the car is perpetually filthy. The dogs and cats love it.

We have seen a lot of Bryony and family, who after our move were galvanised into action and within weeks had sold their house and bought a bungalow (also not without considerable ups and downs) in Droitwich Spa, a very pleasant small town with excellent access for wheelchair users and the famous brine baths. It is a pleasant half-hour cross-country journey from here (no horrible motorways) and also good for Ray to get to work. (He doesn't mind the motorways). They will be out of their house by Christmas and if not into the bungalow, they will be with us. Tristan is still very small and light for his age and has to make regular trips to hospital for inconclusive check-ups, but he is a most cheerful, amusing baby, just starting to walk, and, of course, we love him to bits.

As for other family news, Barnaby flew home for the wedding

not long after he started a new job with United Nations in Nairobi, Kenya, after a very traumatic end to his fifteen-month stint in Rwanda with Oxfam. His Rwandan girlfriend is now living with him and teaching French at a school in Nairobi, and he seems well content with his life there.

Richard now has four little grand-daughters, two of whom are in Jakarta where Dave works for Unilever, and two in Paris, so, alas, we don't see much of them. Just occasional brief visits. William came out of his year-long Buddhist retreat and has gone to Japan to earn enough money teaching English to pay for a three-year retreat on Arran. At one stage he was doing two thousand prostrations a day, and for long periods he was simply meditating, all to eventually gain inner happiness. We had some interesting conversations, but I fear we fail to understand.

Belinda returned safely from her lone expeditions in the Andes but found it difficult to get the sort of job she wanted. After several months she found a short-term job with a computer Internet company in London, and was soon offered the job on a permanent basis. She turned it down, wisely we think, as the hours and conditions were appalling, despite its prestige and pay. She is going freelance now. The working world seems mad to us. No fun at all.

There is no holding back my father. Aged eighty-four he travelled alone (on a package tour) to Sri Lanka, where he met a marvellous sixty-five-year-old on the back of an elephant (where else?) and now they take off all over the place, Paris, Malta, the Western Isles. Sarah lives in Scotland so they alternate visits to each other's houses, enjoying each others company, and he is to spend Christmas and Hogmanay with her. He is sure he will live to be a hundred, and as he is always right, no doubt he will.

Now, on with the unpacking of all the boxes still in the store, and the decorating and painting of the house, and the preparations for Christmas. If you get a chance to come and see us, you would be very, very welcome.

With love from us both

Upper House back door

Upper House

Christmas 2000

Dear ——

A happy and interesting year! Very family orientated, but with enough space to get on with our lives as well.

Bryony, Ray and Tristan came to live with us before last Christmas, not knowing how long it would be before they could move into their bungalow. It was not an easy time for any of us, but we survived remarkably well for the two months they were here. Ray's mother came too for Christmas and New Year. Her husband had died the previous Christmas. We spent New Year's Eve at home, and opened the windows at midnight to hear the Suckley church bells ringing across the fields.

I'm not quite sure why I bought a Red Setter puppy for Richard's birthday in January. When I met Richard he had Seamus, a beautiful and sensible red setter, and now I'm trying to disprove the popular belief that they are all scatty and stupid. Rufus (known as Goofy Roofy) is not entirely brainless, and he *is* very handsome, elegant and completely amiable.

On moving here, we thought we would just mow lawns and keep a low maintenance garden, but in the spring we got enthused, and have spent many happy hours and pounds on reviving and creating the garden, clearing beds buried under nettles and bindweed, digging up hideous old concrete paths, re-fencing the paddock and the pond (now dug out, lined and brimming), chopping down trees, and planting the paddock with woodland shrubs and trees. Richard mowed paths there which wind among the uncut areas which make such a good habitat for voles, and one day, perhaps, barn owls, and an exciting playground for the dogs.

In March we had another Barnaby Experience, (the first was Cambodia) in Africa. In January he became engaged to Chantal, who taught him French when he was in Rwanda, so we were meeting her too. On arriving in Nairobi I was unnerved by his first remark when meeting us in his four-wheel drive vehicle. 'If anyone comes up to the car and say they like it, and they have any sort of weapon in their hand, you just get out and let them have it.'

We were mightily impressed by Chantal, their lifestyle, his office in the huge and amazing United Nations compound and Africa and Africans in general, but not by the necessity to lock all car doors when driving and to be bolted and barred into our bedroom at night in his spacious and stylish bungalow where a guard patrolled all night and there was an alarm button by our heads. We couldn't go for a walk on our own, and all the 'safe' shopping areas (very sophisticated too) had guards with guns.

We visited excellent museums and Barnaby and Chantal took us on two safaris. (We thought we had seen it all on TV—wrong again) which were mind blowing, and so was the traffic on the roads, where hardly one vehicle in a thousand would have passed an MOT. Barnaby's driving was extremely skilful as we hurtled past huge potholes, ragged road edges, buses coming crabwise, bicycles and people.

Naturally, we discussed wedding plans, and discovering that the bridegroom pays in Africa, they thought it would be easier to be married in England and to have a small wedding with close relatives, and so I offered to host it here. It was supposed to be a stressless event. The wedding had to be in August because of their leave, which did not leave a lot of time, especially as communications between here and Nairobi are not easy or always reliable. I did the research and they made the decisions and then I fixed it!

We planned to have the reception here in the old cider house (an open-sided barn) after the ceremony in Suckley church (choir, bells, etc.). The rector had lived in Africa, is married to an Indian, and speaks Swahili (one of the several languages that Chantal speaks) We are disappointed that he has now left to become a bishop in Tanzania, as we liked him very much.

I became increasingly anxious as numbers grew (to over sixty) that we could not fit everyone under cover if the weather was bad, and we had no contingency plans. Getting visas for Chantal's family was a nightmare and an uncertainty until one week beforehand. I wrote letters to numerous African embassies guaranteeing support for various relatives and friends and in the end only her mother, two brothers, one of her sisters with a six-month-old baby, and an uncle could come.

Barnaby and Chantal arrived three weeks before the day, and we had hoped to show them the wonders of Worcestershire, but they spent so much time on the phone and fax, finalising details that this did not happen. A pity, as Chantal had not been to England before. They did manage brief visits to London (shopping for wedding suit, etc.) Edinburgh and Glasgow. Chantal is a city girl!

Our house was full (good helpers all) and so were the local hotels and B&Bs as they do not abound in this non-tourist area. The weather was glorious the whole weekend (I think they were both surprised how good the weather can be and Chantal was amazed at the lack of security—and servants). The plans came together to make it a very special and memorable day.

They had a few days honeymoon in England and the day before flying back, they bought a house (for security) in nearby Bromyard, to be let for the present. So from being involved with clergy, caterers, and choirmasters all summer, we have moved on to house agents, solicitors, and financial advisers all autumn. I was forced to go onto e-mail (but am only a one-trick dog) and it has made things much easier, though often accompanied by gnashings of teeth (still my own) and fiendish frustration when things go wrong on the computer.

We helped to move Bryony and Ray into their bungalow (the sheep trailer comes in handy for this sort of thing) and see them, and have Tristan to stay, on a regular basis. He goes to something called Music Monsters (not Music *for* Monsters) and is a keen joiner in with anything going, although rather smaller than most of his mates. He has a definite ear for music (well he always jiggles about when the Archers comes on) and is still the biggest smiler and comic we know.

Bryony has a selection of wheelchairs and an electric scooter and a marvellous gadget on the roof of her car which enables her to get into the car without help as it grabs the wheelchair from beside the car door and takes it up onto the roof.

They have also had various alterations done to the house, and an *en suite* built on to their bedroom to make things easier for her. She copes remarkably well and has no help except a cleaner twice a week and a physio, and I should think she is a well known sight in Droitwich as she takes the dog out with Tristan perched on her knees on the scooter.

We spent a good weekend recently in Paris (going by Eurostar) with Marc and Sophie and their two little girls, honing our grandparenting skills, and another in London, combining a visit to Andy and Natasha (hoping to be able to get out of London soon) and helping Belinda to move into her new flat (she is just starting a new job). We squeezed in a visit to the Tate Modern which is the nearest I have got to any painting this year (apart from the decorating kind). Nicola and Dave are still in Jakarta and rent what looks like a small palace on the video, but apparently the sun hardly ever gets through the smog and Dave has to work incredibly hard.

William is teaching English in Japan until well into next year, and has already put his deposit down for his three-year retreat in 2002.

Matthew and Jenny are expecting a baby in April and so are Barnaby and Chantal so we are on Spring Standby.

We have managed a few mini trips in the caravan, greatly enjoyed by us and the dogs.

I have joined the WI and Richard continues with cookery. He came off the Prozac after Africa and has put on an unbelievable two-and-a-half stones in weight (actually overtaking me!).

We are involved with a local history group, are learning French conversation (in six weeks I have not spoken one word! Is this the teacher or is it me?) have got to know nice neighbours and frequent excellent concerts and plays in Malvern. We thought the summer was good and we played croquet on the carefully tended lawn with the millennium croquet set intended as Richard's (only) birthday present before I saw the advert for Rufus.

We were untouched by the fearful floods although they were within two miles of us and prevented us getting Tristan home for three days because the rivers Teme and Severn are between us and Bryony and the roads and bridges were unpassable for miles.

My father has had a happy year with Sarah, whom we like very much indeed. They have seen each other throughout the year and had holidays in England and abroad.

Last week he announced that he was leaving his house (promised for many years to Ann and myself) to the grandchildren, and removing the responsibility of being executors from us. I mind the latter more than the money. I make no comment! We're going up to see him before Christmas so we may find out why.

I'm really looking forward to Christmas this year, having decided to do absolutely *nothing*. We're giving only to children (and those on the way) and not expecting any presents ourselves. I am not decorating (well, perhaps a few sprigs of our holly), not cooking, no puddings, cake or turkey, not having anybody to stay, in fact hibernating. Bryony has invited us for Christmas dinner, which will be super, and that will be it. After all, we have had three weddings in four years and other celebrations and events, and I feel I need a break. I wonder if I will regret it? I'll let you know next year.

All good wishes for your own special Christmas, and love from us both.

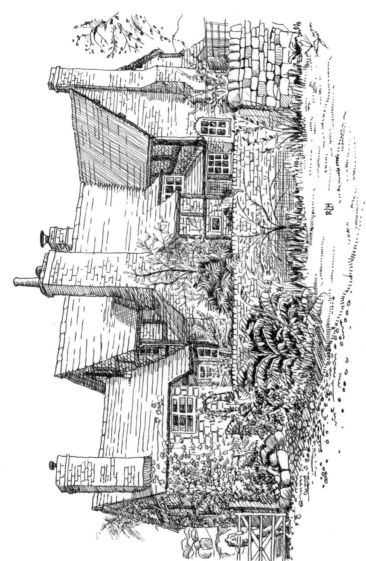

Upper House front door

Upper House

Christmas 2001

Dear ——

Last year's very quiet Christmas went according to plan and was entirely successful except that Bryony delivered a bombshell by announcing that she was pregnant again, thus leaving us plenty of time to worry about how she would manage. More of that later.

Then Foot and Mouth hit the country and dominated our lives for months. We were convinced from the first week that mass vaccination was the only sensible answer, and we grew increasingly angry, outraged and despairing that nobody was taking any notice of our many letters, e-mails and faxes to newspapers, radio and Tony Blair, although several were printed. Recently we have read an excellent and serious report on the crisis by *Private Eye*, which explains clearly all the hidden details behind the political scene. We surfed the net every day for information, and went on an organised demonstration outside the MAFF office in London. Unfortunately, it was not too well supported and we were outnumbered by police and press! Afterwards, a trip on the London Eye cheered us up before catching the train home.

Foot and Mouth came to farms two miles from us and we daily feared and dreaded finding the Ministry men at our neighbours' farms, the milking herd at the bottom of our lane, the beef sucklers at a friend's farm and the superb herd of pedigree Herefords down the road. The tales of brutality and cruelty made us utterly sick and totally disbelieving that this could happen in Britain. And not mentioning the effect It has had on so many other industries.

To take our minds off all this, Jenny and Matthew's baby was born in early April. Joyous news and we rushed up to Glasgow to see Oliver (appallingly sinister smoking fires all up the Eden Valley). Jenny and Matthew had planned a quiet bonding week before calling in the grandmothers, but the plans fell apart when

Jenny had a caesarean op, and the baby's leg was broken in getting him out. They came home a very few days later, with Oliver's leg strapped to his body which made it difficult to change him, and impossible to bath him. His navel became infected, and so did Jenny's womb. I stayed to help, and went again later.

Jamie Bitenyo Jones was born a month later, also by caesarean section, as he was stuck. Through the computer we were able to see photos of him almost straight away. It is not politically correct to call him a mixed-race baby. We now say dual nationality, and Barnaby assures me that in Africa he would be known as 0.5. Just thought you'd like to know!

Carenza Lauren (a Cornish name) was born in August, and Bryony had a quick and easy labour, and I stayed with them for nearly two weeks. Bryony has been truly delighted with the baby and has coped really well, and after six weeks of full-time family help, is now supported by the Social Services who allotted her fifteen hours a week, during which a rota of people help in any way that she needs. Carenza has not needed the special care that Tristan had and is eating and growing well. In fact, at four months old, she weighs half what Tristan does at three plus. Not long before she was born, he went in for an operation to close a valve in his heart which perhaps accounted for his tiny appetite and light weight. Despite his size, he is a most engaging little chatterbox, and came with us in the caravan for a few days in Dorset, enjoyed by us all. The African family came for a fortnight in August, which was fun, but exhausting. We find the ways of today's parents rather puzzling, to say the least. And they are always asking, 'How on earth did you manage with four?' Keeping the grandmotherly mouth tightly shut, I mutter, 'Well, it was different then.' And how!

The garden and new greenhouse gave us pleasure and consolation in spring, and we hosted a cream teas and croquet afternoon for the local history society to raise money for it, as we all hope to publish the information we are getting slowly.

I was press-ganged into being the treasurer of the WI as there were no volunteers, and I'm on a steep learning curve, as I gave up maths when I was twelve, and have been somewhat indifferent to figures and numbers ever since. We finished with the college French lessons and found private tuition with a fascinating woman who acted as interpreter to NATO in Brussels after the September eleventh catastrophe, and was whisked away in a helicopter to an RAF plane.

Richard managed a weekend at the Grand Prix with Ray in the caravan while I stayed with Bryony in case the baby arrived. He also sailed on the Broads with his cousin for a week in September and I stayed in the caravan nearby and painted and walked the dogs, and explored, and enjoyed the break from the babies!

Eleven days in Cornwall, a week at Windy Ridge (rather weird, but wonderful) where we helped Matthew and Jenny move house and office to Kendal (hurray!), a four-day visit to Oxford organised by the Oxford WI, and other short breaks makes me feel I have hardly been here. Natasha and Andy have moved out of London to Great Missenden, and Barnaby and Chantal have also moved out of central Nairobi to a spacious bungalow where the area is patrolled by guards and dogs.

Richard fell off a ladder while converting our little stone barn to a desirable residence for rehabilitating barn owls, and severely bruised his ribs and body (spectacular colours).

He continues with the cookery lessons, and when we have visitors he provides most of the main meals (fantastic).

Belinda was made redundant earlier this year. She is going for an interview soon so we keep our fingers crossed for her; Nicola and Dave, Isobel, now five, and Olivia, now two, came back from Jakarta, but Dave has now got a top job with Unilever in Brussels. Sophie and Marc, Lily, who is four, and Clara, who is two, were hoping to move to the country round Paris, but Marc has been depressed and off work, so things have not been easy for them. William is in retreat again, for six months, and hopes to do a three-year retreat after that. He doesn't want news, only fruit cakes.

With all these grandchildren I was keen to buy a playhouse, but Richard spotted a beautifully decorated real gipsy caravan (wagon) which now gives us as much pleasure as it does the children, and Richard sometimes lights the stove and we have 'gipsy teas' in it (and sometimes without the children).

Unhappily, my father is seriously ill at this moment. After a recent holiday in Morocco with Sarah, his health deteriorated suddenly, and he now looks his eighty-seven years instead of the vigorous sixty-seven as before. He is in hospital having tests, and we cannot make plans until we know the results, Sarah has been staying with him, and has been absolutely wonderful. He is philosophical about his illness, does not want prolonged and possibly ineffective treatment, feels he has had a good life, and doesn't care if this is it (his words). Good for him. We have often said 'Roy is *amazing*'. He has never complained about anything and always has boundless enthusiasm. He justifiably adores Sarah, and has been so fortunate in these latter years.

All this year's batch of babies and their parents are coming for Christmas. I know it will be chaotic, but I hope it will also be fun.

Best wishes for a lovely Christmas and a very happy 2002.

Upper House vegetable garden

Upper House

Christmas 2002

Dear ——

Looking back at this year's calendar to remind myself what has happened, I find rather a lot of appointments with doctor, dentist, physio, hypnotherapist and a consultant. Signs of getting old! But at this moment we are on our feet and still smiling, and in general it has been a good year for us.

Not a single baby has been born in the family, although another one is on the way in Kenya, and family have inevitably occupied much thought and time.

In fact, it has been a fairly undramatic year, apart from the death of my father ten days before last Christmas. Barnaby and family had just arrived and I was in the middle of preparations before the others descended on us. We sped north to stay with my sister who lives near Blackpool and my father.

Roy died in hospital of cancer of the bladder which had begun when he was in Morocco with Sarah in the autumn. He had very positive ideas on death and dying and had long ago left his body for research. Sadly, Liverpool University could not accept his body, so Ann and I sent him off to be cremated, as instructed by him, without any kind of funeral at all, which most people seemed to think very strange.

What he wanted was a family gathering near his August birthday, so Ann and I rented a large house near Sedbergh for a weekend. Our families stayed in the house (caterer provided) and on the Saturday we invited his friends and family for lunch. We made up an exhibition of his life and a speech or two. All very successful.

The week before, Richard and I had been on holiday with Bryony, Ray and the children at the Calvert Trust in the Lake District, which runs activity holidays for disabled people. Our job was to look after the children and feed the family in the self-catering accommodation while Bryony went riding, sailing, abseiling, etc. with the help of Ray. Unfortunately, we picked up a ghastly bug one by one. Richard spent his days struggling down to the one washing machine (used by thirty-six people) which was generally occupied even in the night! By the time we got to Sedbergh I could eat little and drink less. But the cousins rediscovered each other, and we felt we had finally laid Roy to rest.

My father had changed his will back to Ann and me, and the sale of his house went through speedily (an awful business packing up someone's whole life), and I am putting the money into the conversion of the hop kiln here so that the family can stay there and be rather more independent of us. Could this be the result of last Christmas? As predicted, it *was* fun, but also *very* hard work.

In January I went to Denman College with a bursary from Suckley WI, owned by the WI, for a four-day stone carving course. A complete switch off from all household humdrum. I returned with a relief carving of barn owls for Richard's birthday. The real thing has been something of a disappointment. The pair laid and hatched out eggs, and after feeding them for a couple of weeks as usual, the entrance was opened and the parents flew to freedom. They should have come back to their babies, but didn't, so Richard fed them himself until they too flew, and although they have been sighted by a neighbour, the dream of watching them hunting in the gloaming has not materialised.

I was diagnosed with a rapidly growing cataract in one eye more than a year ago. In March I saw a consultant and on the NHS I would have to wait at least another six months for the operation, going private, I was in the hospital in four days! I opted for long sight in that eye (not previously aware that one could choose,) and the op took a mere ten minutes under local anaesthetic. I had imagined that one would be strapped down to prevent voluntary or involuntary movement, but no, the thought of joggling the needle or knife as it goes into your eye is a most powerful deterrent, and of course, I felt nothing and saw little. So now I have the strange mixture of one short sighted eye and one long sighted eye. I was told that I would adapt and I have, sometimes managing without specs at all.

The caravan has been well used, travelling to Derbyshire, the Gower, Shropshire, and Anglesey, with and without Tristan and/or the dogs. Richard took to the woods in it for a nine-day greenwood course, and came home with a beautiful stool and a chair.

We visited Nicola's newly acquired villa in Menorca, and flew to Canada in August to travel over the Rockies and into Alaska by coach, train, helicopter, raft, cruise ship and horse. Saga has the reputation of being for the old and wrinkly, but you have to be an extremely fit old and wrinkly to keep up with all they plan for you. It is not really our scene, being out and out tourists and the luxury was rather obscene, but it was a fascinating experience.

Everything in the garden grew and grew, sunflowers fourteen feet tall with enormous heads, lots of vegetables, and fruit this year. We continue to dig ourselves in to local society, holding another cream teas and croquet afternoon for the history society, and hosting the WI garden party for about sixty people. Suckley WI is closing down as no one came forward to be president at the AGM. I was willing to carry on as treasurer, though my aptitude for money and maths did not improve much in the last year.

Tristan is now in full time school (from four years and four days) so we do not, alas, see him so much. Children's weekends seem to be occupied with partying on a scale which makes one wonder what will amuse them when they are ten, fifteen and twenty. The benefit though has been a noticeable drop in the colds we had last year, which were almost continuous and very virulent.

Silver, our eleven-year-old collie, died rather suddenly of bone cancer, which was a horrible shock, as she was only slightly lame when we took her to the vet. I fear I cried more over poor Silver than over either of my parents, which is pretty sad in itself. Eventually, we decided to give a home to a rescue collie, but Daisy crossed our path, she is a long-legged, smooth-haired collie/lurcher, which in these muddy fields is perhaps a little more sensible. She was not good with cats so we embarked on a long-term rehabilitation programme including dog training classes (much more entertaining to me than watching toddlers at Tumbletots!). Rufus loves her. Poppy tolerates her, and the cats ignore her, not appearing to realise her lethal qualities. The woman who took her in and nursed her badly broken leg, had sixteen greyhounds living in her hoouse, waiting for new homes. It made me feel quite sane.

We keep a toe in the farming world, feeding a neighbour's hens, and checking cattle when a farmer friend was away, and Richard helped to get some of the harvest in next door, but we don't regret not being more involved. It seems no fun at all these days.

Having had visits from or to almost all the family (except William, still in retreat for over a year, and he has 'taken the robes' so we think he must be a Buddhist monk now, but as he can't communicate we are not sure, but we are still sending fruit cakes!) we decided to have a really quiet Christmas and we have booked lunch for the first time ever at a restaurant, and that will be *it*. No turkey, no stuffing of it or us, no huge trolley loads of food and drink, and just the tree to decorate on Christmas Eve.

We wish for peace on earth and a most happy Christmas to you Love from us both.

Upper House sitting room

Upper House

Christmas 2003

Dear ——

Well, did we enjoy last Christmas, eating out and on our own? Yes, we did! But at the restaurant we seemed to be the only people with a smile on our faces. The truly ancient, tucking into turkey, and the parents with grudging, grumpy teenagers did nothing to add cheer to the crackers, candles and Christmas pud.

At home we were in the grip of the Severn Trent Water Board, who had based their operations for digging up every road in Suckley, in the field whose entrance is opposite ours. They promised that there would be very little disturbance, and for six weeks only, so we were enraged by the diggers, tractors, cranes, lowloaders, huge lorries bearing tons and tons of hardcore, vans, arc lights, generators, Portakabins, Portaloos, litter, noise and the stench of diesel, and the seas of liquid mud cascading down the lane as they churned up the banks. They departed at Easter, but reneged on their promise to repair the lane and leave things as they had been. They were a gloomy lot too, very unfriendly.

The conversion of the hop kiln began before Christmas too. Our builders made rapid progress every day and were cheerful with it. Instead of an empty shell with a leaking corrugated iron roof, we have a three-storey, four-bedroomed (one is my 'studio'!) house with an authentic hop kiln roof, kitchen/dining/sitting room, a loo, etc. on every floor and views of garden or fields from the windows. All done with my father's money and meant originally for family (and friends of course) and we all love it. The interior is modern and minimalist and I have done an abstract mural on each floor. We are letting it occasionally to local people who need extra accommodation, but not on a regular basis. Been there, done that, and quite a tie.

We had too many holidays this year. Can this be possible when one is retired? For me, yes. In between we had such frantic and frustrating bouts of gardening to keep up with the bountiful fruit, flowers and vegetables, as well as trying to keep up with ordinary living, family crises, supervision of builders, etc., etc. that it became just a hassle. The weather was wonderful but the drought round here went on and on, until the fields were the same colour as the sheep grazing them.

Barnaby persuaded us to go to Africa again at the end of February. In retrospect, it was another marvellous and amazing holiday, but I was sure war would break out and strand us in Nairobi (BA planes were cancelled shortly afterwards), and even more certain that I was sitting next to a terrorist on the way out. Even the crew were frisked in front of us on the way back and the plane was surrounded by the armed army at Nairobi, where Barnaby and Jamie (twenty-two-months-old) joined it for the ongoing flight to the Seychelles. Chantal, heavily pregnant, stayed at home. The crew of the very small plane taking us from Mahe to Praslin had great difficulty getting the door shut!

We explored, swam in sparkling water, snorkelled—well, Richard and Barnaby snorkelled. I did try, but I was happy to look after Jamie, who refused to put his dear little feet on the sand, and sat and slept in his pushchair for hours. Barnaby looked after him magnificently, and only forgot once to change his nappy, and coped remarkably calmly when Jamie was sick all over him on a boat to La Digue, where we travelled in an oxcart under palm trees to glorious beaches and giant tortoises in rather smelly compounds.

Returning to Nairobi we were waited on by servants and locked into our bedroom at night with a guard patrolling outside, and then driven one hundred miles to a country club in a vehicle with unfamiliar automatic gears that Barnaby had bought on the internet from Japan, and had never driven before! The club had its own safari park where you could walk with the animals (lions and elephants were supposed to be excluded) but as a giraffe had recently kicked a man's head in, we had a guide with a walkie talkie and a little stick. Some people thrive on these thrills—me, I was really glad to get back to boring old Blighty. What a wimp!

We were interested to know what Barnaby thought about the possible war in Iraq. He was, in fact, in favour of it, having worked in Cambodia and Rwanda and he felt that no one who had not lived in such places could really understand what it was like to live under such a regime. He is now assisting the chief of administration of the UN in Nairobi and is going for a week to Namibia for a course and training on AIDS in the workplace.

After that, we went off to Anglesey, France, Devon, West Wales and finally Blackpool, all in the caravan. I had promised Isobel, seven, that we would take her to see the illuminations and the tower circus which I remembered as a child, where the floor sinks down and the ring fills with water and fountains play. We took Tristan, five, too, and apart from getting locked in a lavatory (with the children) on the wild, wet, dark and deserted promenade while waiting for a tram, we all enjoyed it, and fortunately for me, the floor still sinks, and there are mermaids as well.

Natasha split up from Andy (and came to us for a while) both declaring that they still loved each other (we don't understand this!) and she has rented a small house in Leamington Spa, and goes to a pre-uni course for a year before going on to university, which she opted out of before.

Matthew and Jenny have had a really tough year, both going into hospital, Matthew for an anal fissure operation (sounds horrendous) and Jenny with a miscarriage that went so horribly wrong that she very nearly died. Sadly, since then she has had another. As they both work in their business and have no help (Oliver, two, goes to nursery four days a week) the two grandmas rallied as much as they could.

Bryony copes really well with Tristan and Carenza, two, and has a rota of three people to help at key times of the day. She swims, goes to the gym, and is on the equivalent of beta interferon at last, and has to inject herself every day. She hopes it will stabilise the MS and reduce attacks. She felt confident enough to go to Spain this year, which they all enjoyed, apart from Carenza nearly drowning in the swimming pool.

They all came for a family weekend during Barnaby's visit in September. Chantal had a baby girl in April, Sacha Tesi, again by caesarean section, and they stayed in the Hop Kiln, sleeping and eating breakfast there and spending the day with us, which worked well.

William is now a Buddhist monk and wears maroon robes. He is helping to build another retreat on the Isle of Arran, into which he will go for several years when completed. He came to see us in the summer. Belinda is enjoying her job as art director in St George's Hospital in Tooting (where the royal baby was) which is so good as she was unemployed for months. Sophie's job in Paris is in jeopardy, and Marc's Hepatitis C has flared up again and he is off work. Nicola and Dave are back in London in their semi-detached house in Teddington which is now worth at least three quarters of a million pounds. They spend all their holidays in their villa in Menorca.

Our nine grandchildren can be the most delightful company, but we do find them hard work! We do not seem to be alone in thinking there is a nationwide lack of discipline (as we knew it), and the most spectacular waste of food. Our three dogs can hardly cope with the rejects and leftovers. Potty training starts so late, and putting the disgusting nappies in the dustbin must be one of the most unhygienic aspects of this fanatically health and safety conscious age. And they go to bed so late!

Richard made another splendid chair on a second greenwood course, and continues to be chairman of the local history society. He has been depressed again recently, and feels he has no role, although he is a tremendous support to me. Perhaps it is a retirement syndrome, or SADS. Fortunately, the pills work and the doctor is very sympathetic.

My sculpture class at Malvern College (one afternoon a week) is excellent and I made a head of Richard, cast in concrete and burnished with shoe polish to make it look like bronze! And two small nude figures. The latest model has rings and tattoos in interesting places, and fascinating ribbons, wools and plaits in her hair. The previous one was very pregnant and gave birth to her baby shortly after the last class.

On this reasonably cheerful note I wish you all a very happy Christmas and year ahead.

With love from us both.

Upper House kitchen

Upper House

Christmas 2004

Dear ——

The year of *the* birthday—my sixty-fifth to be precise, I didn't feel like a party at sixty, and I might not last until seventy (well, you never know) so I had one in the summer.

Very happily all my family were able to come, though we were sad that of Richard's family, only Belinda was with us. So good fun, house full, food by Waitrose and weather kind. We had worked hard in the garden and were only slightly distracted by Barnaby and family in the Hop Kiln for the fortnight before!

However, I am quite ready to hand over these family gatherings to someone else—when you look in the mirror and first you look like your mother, and then you look like your grandmother, it's no wonder you begin to feel old!

The 'children' gave me a digital camera, which compelled me onto a computer course, which led to Richard going on to one called 'Older and Bolder' and then both of us going together to 'Setting up a Rural Business' which we aren't doing, but is supposed to further our ability to understand the technological age we find ourselves in. I really feel we were happier BC (before computers) and while acknowledging the miraculous things one can do (but only with the instructors at one's elbow!) they more often lead to gnashings and very nearly smashings at home.

Richard gave me six hens and a henhouse at Easter, an early birthday present, as I had decided that enough was enough and we had been without hens for too long. Three hybrids and three rare breeds, so we have eggs and elegance, and even better, a very kind friend who looks after them when we are away—an absolute necessity. The dogs could have been a problem, but a brief encounter with the electric netting which made their run, convinced the dogs that hens have magic powers, even when they now run free.

Richard went sailing on the Broads with Cousin Mike in April and I stayed in the caravan, writing my memoirs! It may be of interest to children and grandchildren one day, to read how we were brought up (so very differently to today.) I had just got to age ten when I was struck down with diverticulitis, and strangely (considering our excellent diet generally) so was Richard in the summer. He spent three days in hospital, which made us think about living here on our own. Not easy and not nice. We now have a large ride-on mower so that I could cut the lawns if Richard couldn't.

The Hop Kiln was useful for neighbours who burnt their house down with a flame gun (yes, honestly and they had only bought it that morning to burn off paint), so they lived here for five weeks before moving into more permanent accommodation, poor things.

Bryony is planning a big extension to her kitchen and some bedrooms, which is both stressful and stimulating for her. The children are either at school or nursery so we have them both for one weekend a month, which we all enjoy. After Holly the dog died, she wanted another, but knew that coping with a puppy was impossible, so she applied to Dogs for the Disabled. Eventually Mack turned up. He is a magnificent Labrador retriever, a fully trained guide dog who went to a blind person, but proved to be an incurable scavenger. (I had a vision of the poor chap sitting down for a meal), Mack is a perfect gentleman of a dog but he does eat anything, including the skin of pumpkins and the dried peas and seeds and the paper of one of Tristan's pictures. They all love him, even Ray.

Bryony was desperate to have a holiday in guaranteed sun this year, and we volunteered to go and help by entertaining the children and giving Bryony and Ray some time on their own. We travelled independently to the west coast of France (in August and by the coast) to a campsite supposedly suitable for a wheelchair user. We arrived as planned on the Saturday, but they arrived on the Wednesday evening exhausted, because just as they were setting off on the Friday to catch the boat, they discovered that Tristan's passport had run out. Ray had to fly to Belfast to get the new passport (the first appointment anywhere in the UK) on the Tuesday, and we left on the Saturday. They stayed for another week and managed, but the site was not good tor Bryony (slippery steps up to the swimming pool, etc.) and we were hardly any use at all. Sad.

Eight friends from Grasmere came to stay in June, for the first Elgar Festival in Malvern. All very successful and jolly, until Richard was caught by a speed camera after an uplifting performance of the *Dream of Gerontius* (my very favourite music) in Worcester Cathedral, at 10.30 pm, travelling at 35 mph. These cameras have had a salutary effect on a lot of people it seems!

Matthew and Jenny have been going through the long process of trying to adopt a baby. When we adopted Natasha thirty-four years ago, we didn't tell anyone until the forms were filled in, the questions answered, the social workers had visited, and the deed was done. Now you have to go on courses, be continually assessed, find people who are willing to be interviewed and fill in forms, and if you are likely to play a part in this possible child's life, to be investigated by the police. I am happy to report that we are not on any police record of convictions, cautions, reprimands or final warnings! Matthew and Jenny have yet to go before a panel to hear if they are suitable. I do hope so.

Recently we went to see Natasha who is now a student at East Anglia University, studying English literature and creative writing. She lives with Jim (they talk of babies, so it must be serious) in a picturesque lodge house near Norwich. She asked us if we ever thought about death. I replied, very promptly, 'every day'. Well, one does, doesn't one? Or perhaps you don't, I'd like to know. We remain mainly cheerful and cautiously optimistic. Richard is on his pills again which helps!

He goes to singing, and lip-reading too—he's only deaf in one ear, so he can cheat a bit, but it may be very useful one day! I love the sculpture class, but embarking (no pun intended) on a life size sculpture of Rufus the red setter is beginning to seem unwise.

The real dog, Daisy, the lurcher-cross-collie has cost us this year. One small tear in her flank and a complete anaesthetic, blood test, x-ray and six stitches later cost £285. In the good old farming days, a squirt of purple antibiotic spray would have healed it in no time. Not long after, she tore a shoulder ligament, and we parted with another £144. She is the only insured pet so it actually cost us £110. One is completely in the vets' control.

We plan to take the caravan and the dogs to a small rural site near Oxford for three nights over Christmas. Walks in the country and a stroll round the bright lights and possibly the midnight service in one of the beautiful churches. Great!

Upper House kitchen

Upper House

Christmas 2005

Dear ——

Last Christmas in the caravan with the dogs was a great success. On Christmas Eve we rode around Oxford on top of a tour bus (without the dogs), went to the midnight service in Christ Church, walked in the frosty fields on Christmas Day, and enjoyed a cosy mini turkey and plum pudding meal in the van on a quiet site (only us there) in a hamlet near the river.

We are approaching our twenty-fifth wedding anniversary so we plan to celebrate by spending Christmas in Venice, in a central B&B, but so far have not found anywhere to eat on Christmas Day. I have a vision of being marooned by floods in our bedroom with a bit of bread and salami. We have been advised to take our wellies!

As for activities, my sculpture class gives me much pleasure, and I did a life-sized model—cast in concrete—of Rufus the red setter. I wasn't pleased with the result, despite the effort, and was delighted when a red setter lover wanted to buy it. I'd have liked to offer her the original, as poor old handsome Rufus has not captured my heart, but he would have to go to a really good home.

We have been to more computer courses, which has meant a new computer and monitor for me and frequent expensive calls for help to the local guru, who had his own problems as his workshop caught fire and destroyed everything he had built up over eight years. It has been an absolute necessity to have a computer, etc. each to avoid divorce. Richard has got very keen, but our methods of getting to the same point are completely different!

With my digital camera I am compiling an album of the garden throughout the year, mainly so that in future years we can remember what we achieved (I will not say in our prime as after a good session in the garden you can hear the bones creaking a mile away.) The ride-on mower has been a big help and Richard whizzes round the lawns and paddock paths. He also whizzed down a bank and through a fence when mistaking the accelerator for the brake. He is now the volunteer footpath warden for the parish, and gets glowing reports in the parish magazine because no one else would take the job.

The six hens I had for my birthday have kept us in eggs, with some to spare, and even moulted in succession which kept the supply going. The compost heap has benefited too.

I had another cataract operation and this time opted for a short sighted lens in my left eye, with which I can read in bed, and with the right I can see distant objects. I do wear glasses to balance things up when necessary (like driving) but if I lost or broke them I could still see, so no need to panic in any circumstance. This operation was done on the NHS and the only difference in care and consideration was that the first was done within six days and the second in six months. Some kind person held my hand throughout this time, and I know it was in case I needed to communicate, but it was comforting too.

Now for the dramas and alarms. Richard was away visiting daughter Sophie in France, and I was expecting to have Tristan and Carenza for the weekend. Tristan had had a bad night with a cough and so they stayed at home. During that night he found it hard to breathe and after coughing up phlegm actually stopped breathing, turned blue, etc. Bryony gave him mouth-to-mouth resuscitation while Ray phoned for an ambulance, which came within a few minutes and he was rushed into hospital in true *Casualty* mode where a team of doctors and nurses revived him and a doctor sat by his bed for three and a half hours. Acute severe croup with respiratory arrest was diagnosed. We were all severely affected ourselves. Happily, he has recovered, and seems none the worse. We are much further from ambulances and hospitals than Bryony is, which is a sobering thought.

Barnaby and Chantal, Jamie (four) and Sacha (two) came to

stay *en route* from Nairobi to a new job in Pakistan, in May. He is now the deputy resident representative for the UN in Islamabad. That move was stressful enough and for some reason all his furniture came here first, which involved a lot of e-mailing once they (but not the furniture) had got to Pakistan. Within weeks of arriving, Chantal was back in England, studying English for three months, while Barnaby coped with new job, country, house, nanny, and the children. Most people thought she was mad, but Barnaby supported her completely as she is aiming for a university correspondence course, and has to pass an English exam to do it.

At the end of the course, he flew here with the children and they came here for a much-needed holiday, which we all enjoyed, despite the fact that they were not able to stay in the Hop Kiln as planned because we have a young archivist staying in it for six months which helps to pay the council tax.

On the morning of their departure we heard of the earthquake in Pakistan, but after an anxious time trying to get in touch with colleagues, they decided to all go. Since then he has been incredibly busy. The UN's twenty-storey building has big cracks in it and is not safe, but there is nowhere else to go. His house was undamaged but they have been woken by severe aftershocks. This does nothing for my peace of mind! Last week he met Kofi Anan at the airport, and entertained Mrs Anan for tea. He sincerely admires Kofi Anan, as do most people in the UN. Barnaby was responsible for making sure the visit went smoothly so he must have been anxious too. Before he left us, he went house-hunting again and made an offer on a small house in Bromyard so we continue to be busy with agents and solicitors, and tenants are still coming and going in the first one, which is, of course, his security if needed.

Richard went to a family gathering in Arran in June, to say goodbye to William for four years. Since becoming a Buddhist monk he has been helping to build a retreat in a remote valley there. He will not have any contact with the outside world, and to help with the various practices (like fasting, etc.) he has to sleep sitting up in a wooden box with an open front. I cannot see how any of this is doing anything for anybody.

Not that I seem to be doing much for society, apart from being editor of the Suckley History Society book, which is very, very long in the making.

Earlier this year I decided to order my coffin, because I want to paint it. It duly arrived in a very large anonymous brown cardboard box. It is of white cardboard (strong, I hope!) and as yet is still waiting for me (to paint it!) in my studio in the Hop Kiln (occupied by the archivist.)

A very dear friend died in August and was given a 'green' burial, managed entirely by his family. We were asked if we could transport him to the green field site in our Volvo, which we would have done had we been able to go to the funeral.

Matthew and Jenny were accepted as adoptive parents but so far no suitable baby has been forthcoming. They have been extremely busy buying and moving into a new office on Kendal's High Street, and Oliver (aged four) has started proper school, as has Carenza.

It seems so young to me, but that is the trend, particularly with most mothers working. Even the school hours are extended these days so that mothers can work a full day.

And some children are provided with breakfast at school too. It must seem an awfully long and exhausting day to them. Or am I being too old fashioned for words?

Natasha and Jim parted company, leaving her desperately upset, and needing to find another rented house in Norwich, which she now shares with two girls. There was a brief reconciliation with Andy, which didn't work out, and she is really throwing herself into the university life and working very hard, and writing essays that she e-mails to me for approval, and I barely understand, but with which she gets excellent marks (or whatever they get these days.) She gave up smoking, but all the stress and unhappiness started her off again. She went to help Barnaby out for three weeks in

Pakistan, but the visit was not a success, partly because she didn't like the country, and found the restrictions on women appalling and the men lecherous (thinking she was a Pakistani woman.)

Most of our holidays have been in the caravan, and all connected with family and friends. Having children to stay has taken us to places not normally chosen by us—maize mazes, Cadbury's World (for the fourth time) Sealife in Birmingham, and the Severn Valley Railway, as well as the Bromyard Gala, fossil hunting, open farms, concerts with fireworks, and one of the best, *Joseph and his Technicolour Dreamcoat.* Marvellous.

Ray has had a difficult year on the *Birmingham Mail,* and Bryony worries that he might lose his job (they are making many people redundant due to falling circulation which is common to many newspapers). She experiences a lot of discomfort and pain, which regular visits to the gym and swimming pool alleviate. She rarely complains, but I know it is difficult for her, which is distressing. She is justifiably proud of the children which are a great comfort to her, and as she says, 'They keep me going and feeling normal.'

We have good friends to keep us cheerful, flu jabs to keep us fit, a new house alarm to keep us safe, and at a price, enough oil in the tank to keep us warm. What more could anyone want?

A happy new year to everyone, and love from us both.

Upper House landing and back stairs

Upper House

Christmas 2006

Dear ——

After Christmas in Venice last year (lovely place, lovely weather, lovely lack of tourists) we were gearing up to a family Christmas here until Barnaby said that he and the family in Pakistan would not be able to come, or see us for eighteen months, so we have agreed, with trepidation, to go to Islamabad instead. More later.

We had been told that nothing would be open in Venice on Christmas Day so bought a pizza and a cake to prevent starvation. Midnight mass in St Mark's Basilica was an experience; finding ourselves locked out of our small hotel when we returned was another. We *had* warned the proprietor. 'No problem, no problem!' Advised by a little old couple shuffling by to keep knocking and banging, we managed to rouse the whole street with the proprietor.

On Christmas Day we walked the streets, and despite the *many* restaurants open, decided to retire exhausted to the bedroom, and we ate our Christmas dinner of pizza and cake in bed. Waste not, want not and very memorable.

Before Christmas we took Tristan (seven) and Carenza (five) to see the Russian Ice Stars perform *Sleeping Beauty* in Malvern. This too was memorable as Carenza, with the excitement plus the very winding lanes *en route*, was violently sick on the carpet by the crowded bar while Richard was ordering drinks for the interval. Commanding Tristan to stand and guard it (highly embarrassing for him as people thought he was responsible), I hustled Carenza off to the ladies while Richard found the management. The performance was so spectacular that we decided to stay although Carenza slept in my arms for most of it. And only we can now tell where it happened.

Richard's stepmother sadly died in October last year, thus releasing his father's will trust, which enabled him to buy a new

Volvo estate, and give our old one to Matthew and Jenny. The new one, despite the 203 improvements that have been made to it, is nothing like as good to use or drive. I get such a pang when they come here that no sooner have I kissed them than I kiss the car as well (only half joking!). They love it too, happily.

In a moment of Midwinter Madness, we acquired our fourth dog. I was browsing RSPCA sites on the internet (as one does on dark and gloomy days) when this handsome young collie appeared. Richard failed to squash the idea instantly so I started enquiries and two weeks later, after home visits, etc., we collected him from Hereford. He too was violently sick (over the new car) and has been a challenge (but then so were Daisy, Caspar and Flight). He had belonged to a ninety-two-year-old man (how foolish is that?) who could not cope with him, and had been in kennels with a man who was marvellous with Rottweillers, but perhaps not collies. With endless patience, titbits and much thinking round his problems he has improved enormously and I love him dearly (not so sure Richard does).

Over the Easter period, nearly all the grandchildren came to stay. Some are afraid of dogs, some don't mind, and some love dogs (any dogs because they don't have them) to bits. I could control the dogs for the former, but not the children for the latter. The only casualty (apart from my nerves) was Oliver (five) riding his bike past a rose hedge when Dan jumped up and pushed him into it. Dan thought his cries were play! Fortunately, no harm was done.

There is no avoiding health, or lack of it, these days. Tristan was staying here for a weekend when I noticed red blotches on his toes and legs. Reporting this to Bryony she discovered he had Henoch-Schönlein purpura, which can be serious—no wonder with a name like that—but it faded away and has not recurred so far. He has to have further hernia operations in the spring. He is a tough little boy, but I do worry.

More serious in the long-term is the diagnosis that Richard has Parkinson's disease. So far he only has slight trembling in one leg and a slight rigidity of the facial muscles. The depression he has had off and on for several years, which has been fine with pills, returned. When he began on the Parkinson's disease pills it lifted immediately. Apparently depression appears to go with Parkinson's disease in some cases, and there is a very great percentage of farmers and gardeners with Parkinson's, which must be to do with chemical usage.

I had to have laser treatment on one eye to clear cloudiness after my cataract operation. Wishing I hadn't read what might happen if I was unlucky, I agreed and it made holes in the cloudy bit and now I can drive in the dark again.

The garden has been astonishingly prolific despite the drought and the fact that we have to pay for all our watering, and Alfrick WI held their garden meeting here, which kept me up to scratch with the weeding. I am on their committee—good fun—and have just been elected on to Suckley Parish Council. About time I put something back into the community. The Suckley Local History Society has at last produced a real book, of which we are inordinately proud. I designed the cover, and to help sales *all* our family are getting a copy for Christmas. Excellent holidays in the caravan, each no longer than a week, and some with grandchildren or friends have taken us to delightful places in England and Wales. Four days in a hotel in Jersey with friends were very spoiling and enjoyable.

We bumped off the hens in the autumn. Egg production was poor and shell quality worse, which was to be expected, but *much* worse was the infestation of red mite, which I could not get rid of despite endless scrubbings and sprayings. I am paranoid about mites of any kind, so no more hens. This does make life a bit easier too, especially going away.

Natasha has a new boyfriend, no surprise there! We like him, he is called George and he is ten years younger than she is. He is a teacher, just qualified, and lives with her in Norwich where she is now in her final year.

Bryony's kitchen conversion is at long last almost complete. They have lived without a kitchen, study, utility room, or bathroom for five months, and have washed and washed up in her *en suite* shower room, and eaten and microwaved in the children's bedroom. Now they have a huge modern kitchen, a bigger utility room, new bathroom and an extra bedroom, and they seem to have survived the upheaval.

The good news and big excitement was hearing that Jenny and Matthew had been offered a baby girl for adoption. Since they were told in September it has been an unbelievably long, drawn out and agonising process on the part of the Social Services (which we do not understand), and they are hoping she will be with them for Christmas. They had nearly given up hope. The baby is twelve months old and has been with a foster mother.

So, please think of us in Pakistan! I will be taking a kaftan and plenty of scarves. It will be very cold, much better than too hot. Barnaby wanted us to take crackers, but I have no wish to have even the tiniest amount of explosive found in my luggage! He has plans for sightseeing, but a walk round his garden every day would just suit me fine, as nothing I have read recently about Pakistan reassures me in the least.

A very happy Christmas and love, from homelover of the year (and husband).

The Hop Kiln

Upper House

Christmas 2007

Dear ——

Last Christmas in Pakistan was not what we expected, i.e. no alcohol, freezing weather, and primitive conditions. And no Christmas as we know it. Wrong, wrong, wrong. Severe fog delayed us, but once there it was yet another amazing Barnaby experience, more alcohol than we would have had at home, mild sunny winter weather, and a spacious house with garden, verandah, servants, and a very traditional Christmas.

However! Every house in the neighbourhood has a high wall surrounding it with a guard, we had to keep the downstairs curtains closed so the guard could not see us, and especially me, in or out of bed in our downstairs room, very few women were about anywhere, and the splendid Marriott Hotel where we sang carols round an enormous Christmas tree was the target of a suicide bomber not long after we came home.

We saw the UN office on the fifth floor of a twenty-storey office block where access was by lift only, making it a death trap in an emergency situation like an earthquake! So the UN was building a splendid new office which was causing Barnaby enormous stress for various reasons as he was in charge of the operation, and had very little time off, as of course Christmas is not celebrated by the Muslims. We were invited to excellent parties given by the ex-pat community, and met some most interesting people. Christmas lunch (feast) was at the UN Club, decorated in red, white and green with crackers, balloons and with an array of food and (alcoholic) drink to dream of.

Barnaby managed to take us up into the thirty-thousand-foot Margalla Hills nearby, with its ferociously steep S-bends and views over the city. Driving a vehicle with one hand on the wheel while using a mobile does not seem to be forbidden in Pakistan!

We also drove into the surrounding areas of Islamabad and glimpsed something of the lives of the peoples in the villages. Very different.

Church with Chantal and the family, and visiting the French school where Jamie and Sacha go, were fascinating, and not only because we had to pass through road blocks and barriers manned by armed soldiers to get into the diplomatic compound where they were.

The journey back to UK was grim, delayed for hours by security, and then by blinding rain, crashes on the motorway so no scheduled bus, a complicated train journey and finally a taxi driven by a Pakistani man, which seemed appropriate, to friendly (and safe) old Upper House.

Since that experience, life has been delightfully tame, though far from uninteresting. We had barely been back a week before a completely unexpected thing happened. William rang to say he was no longer Tashi, the Buddhist monk, and no longer in the 'inner' retreat, and would like to come and stay with us the next day. Thankfully, we were not away and met him at Worcester station, hardly recognisable as he was so thin and unkempt. He was with us for three-weeks, during which time we fattened him up on non-gluten food. He told us he was not benefiting from the retreat, missed human contact, and felt the opposite of relaxed. Unfortunately, he also felt a failure and that he had let himself and the community down. The conditions in the five-month inner retreat were very harsh, not speaking, not washing, not eating after lunch time, and having to sleep sitting up in a wooden box. He then went to live with his mother and took a computer course in Bath, before moving to London where he has been looking for a job and living in a Buddhist centre. He came on a wood turning course with Richard in May and took home a rocking chair that they had made together.

Richard's daughter Sophie and husband Marc have had a very tough year in Paris. Marc has been having treatment for drug and alcohol addiction, and they have struggled through all that and then Sophie lost her job and car. As she had enjoyed the job, it was doubly difficult.

In February, Rachel Carrie came into the family, aged eighteen months and adopted by Matthew and Jenny. A really remarkable child, endlessly cheerful, sleeps well, eats well, sociable, and isn't afraid of dogs! Needless to say they are thrilled with her. They stayed over Easter, and we have looked after her and Oliver twice during the year, once here and once in the caravan in the Lake District while Matthew and Jenny went brainstorming together (whatever that means!). I did have to pop her back in the bunk about fifty times until she fell asleep exhausted (not as exhausted as I was.)

Our proper holiday was sailing on the Hurtigruten, which is a working fleet of boats, calling at many ports up the Norwegian coast, from Bergen through the Arctic Circle, delivering goods and people. Expeditions ashore varied from seeing the cathedral at Trondheim to sea eagles up a narrow channel where the whirlpools are spectacular because of the immensely strong current. It was too warm to go dog sledding with the huskies, but a holiday to be recommended. Delicious food too.

I delayed my arthroscopy (keyhole surgery on my knee) until the autumn as we have looked after various grandchildren during the summer. I went into Kidderminster hospital for a day— NHS—and came out with two sticks but no MRSA. It seems the condition of my knee was 'severe' and so it will probably need to be replaced sometime. Not good news as the recuperation takes much longer. Richard coped manfully, but taking all the dogs out for the morning walk is not much fun on your own.

He continues fit, and cheerful (thanks to the pills!), although a little slower. He gave me a hot air balloon flight for my birthday, which I loved, even though we had to get up at 4.30 am. It was the one glorious morning soon after the floods, and we floated over local countryside that we knew well from the ground.

Our house was not affected by flooding, but all roads out were blocked for a few days. A family in Suckley, living in a narrow valley by a stream, had forty minutes to try and rescue belongings before scrambling over the garden fence, up a bank and into the surrounding woods, when the water almost reached the downstairs ceiling. Jason; his wife, Amanda, who was eight months pregnant; and their two daughters came to live in the Hop Kiln, and I was on red alert with my calving and lambing skills, but baby Ben was born safely in hospital and is now nearly three months old, and a lovely lively baby. Their house is almost ready for inhabiting again, and they should be in it for Christmas.

Much of the time since Barnaby and family's hectic visit here in July has been taken up by house buying for them (his money!) in Malvern this time. He has not even seen the house they now own and let to tenants, and it has certainly put me off moving. No pleasure at all and much hassle. While here, he wanted to give the children, now six and four, the caravanning experience, so for two nights we took them into Wales (minus Chantal who sensibly visited her brother in Birmingham). It rained continuously. Barnaby slept outside in a teeny cheapo tent on very lumpy gravel (not allowed to pitch on the sodden grass!) and somehow managed to survive the nights while the rain thundered down. A good time was had by all.

We enjoyed a week in the Yorkshire Dales with friends from Grasmere, and a week on the Gower with Bryony and family, unavoidably, but never again, during the August bank holiday.

We determined to stay at home this Christmas, after gadding about for the last three, so we may or may not be on our own. Either way we shall be happy.

But, of course, I am *not* happy about the situation in Pakistan and rather hoped that Chantal and the children would come here, certainly before the elections, although apparently Barnaby has to stay whatever. We now speak to each other on Skype—

this is a very recent happening and has taken a year and much frustrating time to finally work so I can see them all—and for free. Yet another amazing invention that boggles the brain.

We heartily hope *you* will have a very happy Christmas and we send our love.

My studio

Upper House

Christmas 2008

Dear ——

Christmas last year was rather a non-event, so I will not dwell on it. I had ordered a good sized turkey in case Barnaby and family were with us, but as they weren't we sat on either side of it and enjoyed ourselves. Nicola and her two girls and Sophie and her two girls came soon after and helped to eat the remains. The children wanted me to teach them how to knit and I have a lovely photo of them sitting on the sofa, totally absorbed with needles and wool. They all look like with-it teenagers, but the oldest was eleven!

The following month we travelled to Paris on Eurostar to see and hear Lily (eleven) singing in Mahler's Eighth Symphony (Symphony of a Thousand). Very marvellous indeed.

Not so marvellous was having to go to Hereford County Court to get one of Barnaby's tenants out. I was shocked to find I was swearing the oath on a paperback bible, and tatty at that. The tenants knew the system better than we did and eventually owed him nine months rent which was not worth trying to get back.

But the naming ceremony of Oliver and adopted Rachel, Jenny and Matthew's children, held in a Kendal hotel, was a very happy occasion and a meeting of sisters, brothers, in-laws, grandchildren and ex-husbands.

Barnaby came over in March to help Brian, who is not well and has been persuaded to move to a flat, and then Chantal asked if she and the children could come to live here as the situation in Pakistan had become intolerable. We were only too pleased to welcome her, Jamie and Sacha (who had their seventh and fifth birthdays within a week of arriving) and Elizabeth, the African nanny/help. They arrived in April and lived in the converted Hop Kiln and were more or less independent—except for transport, so in fact we were very involved. I enrolled the children in Suckley school, with its forty-eight pupils, and they made friends and settled in well.

Chantal continued with her university correspondence course and they stayed until August with only a few cultural misunderstandings! which Barnaby helped us all to sort out using his diplomatic skills, when he came for a fortnight's holiday.

The delightful children got excellent reports (and nits) from the school. The reports were not like ours used to be, a simple 'good' or 'could try harder' but an A4 four-page character analysis. I pity the teachers. Jamie and Sacha were christened here a week before they all left for Vietnam where Barnaby was starting a new but similar job with the UN—much to our relief. The Marriott Hotel which was blown up was the one where we sang carols round a huge Christmas tree two years ago.

I knew my left knee needed a replacement, but the main tendon in my right foot ruptured in early spring and the consultant thought he might as well do a complete reconstruction of my foot (on the NHS), but it was a bit unfortunate that I was summoned to the Worcester hospital about six weeks after their arrival. So Richard had to take over the transporting of the children to the school, Chantal to the shops, exercising the four dogs every day, and looking after me, as I was not allowed to put my foot on the ground for weeks. I was warned that it would take a year to mend, so I progressed from wheelchair, to zimmer frame, to sticks, and we bought a second-hand electric scooter so that I could get into the garden, and eventually was able to do some gardening within arms reach. The downstairs bedroom and wheel-in shower room which we put in for Bryony came in useful. I discovered that being in a wheelchair all the time is very hard work, as Bryony knows all too well. Richard was an absolute star, and I have to say I enjoyed having breakfast in bed for six weeks until I was able to hobble about. I am now waiting for the knee op. Above the knees I am fine, just fine!

Fortunately, Richard has kept well, and walked for three days down the Wye Valley with Belinda and Will, has chopped down other people's trees (by request), is the footpath warden here, goes to singing, music appreciation mornings, and decided to join the local keep fit class, only to find that it was a ladies' keep fit class. Naturally this did not bother him (or them, apparently).

Will recently announced that he was thinking of becoming a Buddhist monk again, which dismayed Richard as he remembered only too well the state Will was in last year when he came out of retreat. He wrote him a letter reminding him of that and mentioned the 'mediaeval practices' he had undergone. Will wrote a very nice letter back saying it was too late, he was already a monk (now to be known once more as Tashi).

We used the caravan to go to Ireland for the first time, (really lovely) and have taken the grandchildren in it for brief holidays. Poor Carenza chipped one of her new front teeth in the Droitwich swimming baths, and has had two migraines, aged seven, which seems very early, although they do run in my family, and I have had them since I was thirteen.

Natasha phoned with the good news that she has got her MA with distinction so we are extremely pleased for her as it is the end of five years hard studying. She is living in Norwich with George and they are getting married in February. Hurrah! He proposed in the botanical gardens in Sri Lanka.

I enjoy going to the local WI. The garden afternoon here had to be cancelled because of the awful weather in the summer, which was a shame as somehow we had managed to make it presentable, and I was looking forward to introducing Chantal who wears such beautiful and stunning African clothes.

Now we are rehearsing for a Christmas Entertainment. I am a narrator, which means I can read my lines, so no sleepless nights.

The Credit Crunch is not much fun and Richard worries, but there is no point downsizing, which did appeal when I was disabled, but the thought of sorting and selling is a nightmare. I deeply admire anyone who has faced up to it.

We know we won't be seeing Barnaby at Christmas this year, as they are off to Kenya and Rwanda (where Chantal's mother lives, and whom she hasn't seen for ages) so again we will be having a quiet time. I had no plans to visit them in Vietnam even before I heard they eat dogs there.

Years ago we asked dear Brenda, who left us The Wyke, to come to us for Christmas Day. She replied, 'Thank you, dear, but no. I prefer to share a fish finger with the cat as I don't like all that slaughtering and fuss.' We haven't got to that stage yet, but I can see it approaching. Meanwhile, Bryony and family will be with us on Boxing Day, and Richard's family after that, so we shall make the most of the peace of Upper House on the day in this increasingly violent and worrying world.

Peace and goodwill to you all, with love from us both.

View from the garden of Upper House

Field End
Knightwick Road
Alfrick
Worcs

Christmas 2009

Dear ——

Last year I wrote that we could not contemplate moving, this year we did it. It was every bit as much of a nightmare as we anticipated. But here we are, in a modern bungalow in the centre of a small rural village, tucked away out of sight in a walled garden, feeling that we have 'gone to earth' like a fox in his den or a rabbit in his burrow.

What is good is that we feel we have definitely done the right thing. At the end of January my left knee was replaced and it was back to breakfast in bed and the wheelchair (I didn't feel confident on crutches as my right foot was still recovering from its rearrangement) and the scooter. After a while I was able to rock along Bromyard High Street like a drunken sailor and could even weed in the garden for the WI garden party by imitating a giraffe at a waterhole.

All this prompted more than a few thoughts about the future, which were compounded by a visit from our financial adviser in March, who told us bluntly that we could no longer afford to stay at Upper House with any degree of comfort, or help in the long term—just another victim of the credit crunch.

The very next day I saw an advert in the local paper for a couple wanting a 'period gem' and offering pots of money! I rang the very nice helpful agent and in no time we were on the market, although our period gem was not wanted by that particular couple (who were real people, I have to add).

The day after that (Richard and I do *not* hang about) we went on a preliminary exploration of possible areas to live within a reasonable distance of Suckley as we thought it sensible to still be near family, friends, doctors, dentists, and vet.

Everyone knows you should not look before you sell, but it was by a chance encounter that day that we had a look round the first bungalow we came across, and that was it. Why waste our time looking further?

We had not sold Upper House and certainly did not anticipate the multitude of troubles which lay ahead, with solicitors acting like pit-bulls, obstreperous planners, and British Telecom, who kept changing our telephone number, and even the eventual purchasers who threatened to drop out if we didn't move out at their convenience, which meant moving at very short notice into rented accommodation.

Before all this turmoil, Natasha got married in February, to George in Norwich, only a month after my knee operation, so we took the caravan there so that I could rest when necessary. We really enjoyed it and all my family were there, even Barnaby from Vietnam. Richard was able to do some family research in Norfolk too.

We were so lucky to find Robin Hill, a nice bungalow near a very busy road which meant the cats remained in kennels for three months. I was reminded of the song 'Here we sit like birds in the wilderness, birds in the wilderness, etc., etc.' Us, not the cats.

We took Tristan and Carenza on a long-promised holiday to Mortehoe in the caravan and had a very good week and the weather was as wonderful as our week in Scotland by train, and we returned about a week before we actually moved out of Upper House on 8 July. We travelled on every track and saw Scotland at its best, staying in hotels and not having to worry about anything. Certainly girding our loins for the next few months!

Then Natasha gave birth in August to a baby boy, Rowan Jay (our eleventh grandchild). She suffered a third degree perineum tear (not nice—I looked it up on Google) and we dashed over to Norwich to see him.

Natasha recovered brilliantly and they have already been to stay here (we have a proper guest room with *en suite* and a children's room with bunk beds.)

For the first month here we lived with builders, decorators—how marvellous not to be doing the decorating ourselves for the first time—plumbers, etc. and we have now unpacked the last of the 145 boxes and are hanging pictures and curtains, and of course with downsizing we had money to spend.

I put on weight with all the stress, but after a trip to Ikea and the purchase of a large wardrobe with huge mirror doors, who needs Weight Watchers?!

The dogs now have a 'doggery', a small but useful extension where they sleep in 'bunk beds' and where mud and wellies stay. Actually, Poppy sleeps in our bed since she nearly died after being badly bitten. One can spoil a small dog rotten.

I have a study, where I am typing this, and Richard has a divided off area in the large sitting room, next to the conservatory, and I also have a proper studio up above the garage, which I am thrilled about, and as the garden is comparatively small, I am hoping to get up there quite often.

As for Christmas, we have been invited to Bryony's for the day and I have been asked to provide the games. Barnaby and family will also be there as they are coming to the UK for two weeks, but staying in a cottage as they will be seeing as many of their family and friends as possible. Jamie caught swine flu this year and had to be isolated in his room and wear a mask. A young colleague of Barnaby's died that week and he was responsible for looking after her father who flew out to Hanoi, the funeral, and getting her body back to Finland which included finding a Russian plane which had doors wide enough for the lead coffin. He said it was a very emotional experience.

I was invited to join a reading group in Alfrick, I was already on the Alfrick WI committee, and Richard still goes to the keep fit class with several people who live here, and we received a warm welcome which was much appreciated.

The Dame Laura Knight Society, formed a year ago, has given some interesting talks and outings, and we gave a short talk on 'Acquiring a DLK painting' at the AGM. Only nine people attended so no nervousness was needed!

After a week in the Lake District, partly looking after Oliver and Rachel, and finding that as we got larger, the caravan seemed to get smaller, and it would be something of a blot on the landscape here, we sold it, and will be trying a different sort of holiday next year. We had a lot of fun in the two caravans we owned over ten years, and stayed in wonderful places.

As yet we haven't looked back, either at what we had, or at what our lives were like. I can't imagine how our children would have coped with it all had we stayed there, and I am extremely thankful that we were able to do it together, not by ourselves.

The irony of moving is that one of the reasons we moved was to make life easier, and so far we seem to have worked harder than ever. Perhaps it has been good for us, physically and mentally. Certainly Richard's Parkinson's has not progressed noticeably and my knee and foot no longer need a stick or pain killers and look almost normal. So was the move worth it? I'll tell you next year!

We wish you a very happy and healthy year.

With love from us both.

Autumn at Field End

Field End

Christmas 2010

Dear ——

Our second Christmas at Field End and the downsize has proved to be everything we hoped. Particularly easy on all those bits of the body starting to complain or crumble. Go for it, all those who are dithering about downsizing!

In March we joined HOST, an organisation which connects overseas students at universities here with English families, and enjoyed a weekend with a most charming Chinese girl. For Christmas we are entertaining two girls, one from China and the other from Thailand. We can introduce them to real family life as Bryony and co are coming for Boxing Day.

We exchanged the cumbersome Volvo (hurray) for a versatile Vauxhall Meriva in the spring and have been delighted with it. The boot is more of a squash for three dogs, but no problem for short journeys to the woods or the kennels.

The huge bedroom mirror failed to reduce my weight so I tried Weight Watchers, but as all the helpers were much larger than me and never got any smaller, I gave up and am trying the doctor's dietician.

Natasha announced that George had got a job in Australia, so in June they sold their house, packed up their furniture, and with baby Rowan flew off to Perth in the teeth of the ash cloud. Apart from a redback spider (see Google) in the meter cupboard, all sounds marvellous and the photos are impressive.

Staying a week in Warminster made our most memorable holiday of the year. It sounds unlikely, especially as we had booked in to a wooden lodge on the outskirts and were dismayed to find the wood of the lodge very dark and dismal and our bedroom like a coffin.

But every day we travelled to see a different good friend from the past, who lived in the area, which once we knew well. Seeing them was wonderful and took us down to the coast, on a canal, into Bath, as well as more downsizes, and over countryside redolent with nostalgia. Sadly, we have heard since that two of them have died, but how glad we were to have seen them again.

The unfortunate end of the holiday was arriving home to find the kitchen and surrounding area awash, every light bulb dripping and carpets like bogs. Richard had turned the water off (and I do believe him) and the cause is still a puzzle. Trying to stop the problem, he went into the loft and promptly fell through the soggy ceiling, fortunately getting stuck half way and giving me time to take a photo, have a laugh, and rush to the garage for the stepladder. The industrial dryers blasted away for three solid weeks and the insurers took two months to get us straight again (possibly because we had just changed the company two weeks before).

We had two holidays in the Lake District looking after grandchildren. Determined that Tristan and Carenza, now twelve and nine, should get to know and love it too, we explored the area around Windy Ridge (now used as a holiday cottage by the people who bought it and where we stayed!) We climbed Helm Crag, something of an achievement for my knee and foot, and only possible because of the firm path pitching done by the gang I worked on when I was employed by the National Trust twenty-six years ago. Very meaningful—for me anyway.

Matthew and Jenny have not had an easy year. Jenny had her thyroid removed and was warned she might lose her voice among other nasties, but thankfully this did not happen. Her father has been very ill and has died recently. Matthew's father (Brian, of course) is in a very poor state of health and has been in hospital for three months. Both have necessitated long journeys for them in different directions ,as well as the accompanying worry.

We spent a night in London, attending the annual Arts Open Evening at St George's Hospital, admiring all the work that Belinda has achieved in making it an interesting and people-friendly environment. Richard felt very proud.

He also went to France with his son Will, now known as Tashi, the Buddhist monk. They were tracing the footsteps of Richard's father, who was with the D-Day landings in a field ambulance unit as he was a GP. They went with a group of people, some of whom were ex-soldiers and members of the British Legion and were curious about Tashi in his purple robes, but he very quickly knew all their names and became quite popular.

A coach trip from Alfrick took us to the National Memorial Arboretum near Stafford. We wandered through the extensive grounds by ourselves (not the place for idle chit chat) and all very moving. A hidden garden revealed a memorial for babies either stillborn or those who did not live long, which, of course, affected me deeply.

We are still much involved with the Dame Laura Knight Society in Malvern and have helped to organise walks, talks, and social events. I went down to Penzance with two other committee members for a fascinating weekend with the Lamorna Society which is particularly interested in all the painters who lived around there during the early twentieth century. They are coming to Malvern in May and we shall have to pull out the stops for them.

A big surprise was to hear from Barnaby that his family in Vietnam are coming over in January. Chantal, Elizabeth their help, and the children, will live in Malvern, but Barnaby will return to Vietnam and continue to work in Hanoi after a month. I always knew this was a possibility, but imagined it would be when the children were older. Jamie is nine and Sacha seven and they will go to a school in Malvern, so we hope to see more of them. Sacha, and indeed Barnaby, have been affected by the severe pollution in Hanoi which must have influenced their decision.

I am now secretary of our lively and companionable WI, so my visits to my studio are even less frequent than before, but I still go to my sculpture class which is a discipline I seem to need to do any art. I went on a day's machine embroidery course which I would like to take up, but when?

The WI are putting on a Christmas entertainment this year and I am taking part in three items, not really my scene, but we have a lot of laughs in rehearsals. I am 'singing' a Beverley Sisters song, reading a poem, and in a rather strange nativity as all three kings. Aren't you glad you aren't allowed to come?

There are always sad thoughts at Christmas for many reasons, but we hope most sincerely that there will be happy times and thoughts too.

With much love from us both.

Now We Are Seventy-One
(with apologies to A. A. Milne)

I forget about the Aga
And we have four loos.
I know a ride-on mower
Would never come in handy.
I don't need a greenhouse
And I don't want a cellar.
But oh! Father Christmas, if you love me at all,
I would like a nice, big walk-in pantry.

Well, could *you* make it rhyme!?

Winter at Field End

Field End

Christmas 2011

Dear ———

This has not been the best of years, but it has been sprinkled with good happenings and I will begin with one of them. It was our thirtieth—yes, thirtieth!—wedding anniversary just before Christmas, so we booked in to an eccentric hotel in Evesham (not too far to travel) for a couple of nights. Despite the snow falling and having to walk the dogs the last bit into kennels, we arrived safely. That evening there happened to be a Christmas party, a very jolly and riotous affair with games, balloons, etc. and the owner of the hotel dressed as a fairy with very hairy legs. Surprisingly, a big success. Getting home in thick snow was tricky.

For Christmas we collected the Chinese girl Amy and the Thai girl Lek from the station for three nights and then we were iced in. Bryony and family came on Boxing Day and we played games, introduced the girls to Wii Sport and they even loved the demonstration of the Roomba Robot carpet cleaner. Lovely girls and we think HOST is a really worthwhile organisation.

Early in January Barnaby brought his family to live in their Malvern house. I was thrilled to see them all. We took him to collect a hired car, and alas, he told us they were splitting up. It is a long and unhappy story which has continued as the background to the rest of the year. Eventually, I was told that I had to choose between him and the children, so I have not seen Jamie and Sacha since they all came to visit me in hospital in May. Barnaby is not allowed to bring them here or to see any of the family except Brian who is so ill (with myositis a wasting disease). As you can imagine, it has hit me hard. Richard, the rest of the family, and friends, were very supportive.

I wanted to meet Chantal and discuss what I was doing or had done that was so wrong, but Barnaby told me not to as it would make things worse for him. The only good thing to come out of all this is that they are now attending the private Downs School in Malvern, as day pupils, which is providing a stimulating and caring environment for them. Barnaby is still in Vietnam, but comes to England to see the children as often as he can and has been Skyping them almost every day. Apart from his troubles he says he is fine! No one else is involved in the divorce.

A very happy family occasion was meeting Natasha's 'other mother' Indrani when Natasha, George and toddler Rowan were here from Australia and seeing family and friends from a cottage near Stratford. Natasha asked if I would like to meet her while she was in England seeing her two younger daughters and two small grandchildren. After Natasha's birth, Indrani met and married a German whom she later divorced and is now living in Sri Lanka.

We found them a truly delightful family and found we had a lot in common. Indrani is much involved with the distribution of money and goods to those affected by the tsunami, and she also has five rescue dogs! Both the girls live and work in England.

But before that we had invited my dear sister and husband to stay here and watch the royal wedding with us. We had one lovely sightseeing day with them and Richard cooked a meal for us after the wedding. All was going splendidly until I went to light candles on the windowsill and tripped and fell heavily against the wall. Although in considerable pain (agony!) the men hoiked me onto a chair and the meal continued. Deciding I should go to bed, they somehow got me to the bedroom where I was unable to move. Jack said, 'I think we need help,' and Richard said, 'Let's leave it a bit longer.'

The consequence was: eventually two wonderful paramedics came and with the help of morphine and gas and air got me to hospital at midnight. The neck of the femur was broken so I had a hemiarthroplasty which some of you may know is half a hip replacement. What a complete bore and there was nothing wrong with that hip before.

I am making disappointingly slow progress and still cannot walk more than half a mile (or round our newly refurbished Waitrose) and friends say 'still limping' which I find discouraging.

Our summer was dry, very dry, and we watered all our new shrubs, trees and plants almost every day while listening to reports of torrential rain in Scotland and heavy downpours in the Lakes. The untouchable weeds took advantage and none less than knee high got pulled up.

We were overwhelmed by apples, plums and beans (nothing else is worth mentioning) but so were everyone within miles.

Bryony had her fiftieth birthday and took her family to Majorca for an excellent holiday, and we spent a week in Devon in a totally unsuitable cottage for a person on sticks (steps everywhere and the loo downstairs) and took Tristan and Carenza to Anglesey with surf boards, kites and beach games, but the wind was cold and strong so we went round museums, and castles, and up Snowdon on the railway in the fog, but had a great day with Ann and Jack who were staying with son Adam and family who live on the island.

Our very good friends Andy and Sue sold their house in Suckley at last and moved to Dorset, leaving us bereft. We correspond by e-mail, but it isn't the same as meeting for a coffee or a cuppa and a confidential chat.

Added to all this, Poppy the Jack Russell had been failing since the year began. Eventually she was on more pills than I was (though not Richard). Her heart was leaking and her mind was going—did you know that dogs get dementia too?—among other things. At last the vet was called and she died in my arms here at home. She was a particularly special part of the family and all the grandchildren loved her and would always walk anywhere as long as they could 'hold Poppy'. So I missed her more than I thought possible, but had decided long ago that two dogs were still plenty and we wouldn't have another. However . . .

Sophie and Belinda have new men in their lives, so we are delighted for them. Nicola's friendship with Mark did not survive, and William, alias Will then Tashi, is now Trinley the Buddhist monk. His recent visit was excellent, but I fear we found ourselves reverting to Will again which he said he didn't mind.

Richard thought a puppy would take my mind off the glooms and worries, and I did say 'No, no, no,' but in an idle moment trawling the net (as one does) I found a Jack Russell puppy not too far away. The rest is history and hard work, but she certainly did take my mind off nearly everything else. Happily, we both dote on her which cannot so far be said of the other dogs and cats, although Dan the collie has had some energetic but gentle games with her.

We toy with the idea of visiting Natasha in Australia, but the distance, the cost, and our health daunts us. We enjoy our more local activities and societies and are thankful we can still do them. Our local shop closed this year, but a keen group of people are working towards opening a community shop and we have bought shares and volunteered to help. This has already meant that we have met more local people and as it should be sited within two hundred yards in the grounds of the village hall, would be very convenient too.

We will be thinking of you over Christmas and the new year and send our love and all good wishes for the future.

Spring at Field End

Field End

Christmas 2012

Dear ——

We determined to see the family in the north last Christmas so packing the car with a chicken and a mini pudding and the puppy (safely in a crate) we drove to a log cabin near Ullswater for a week.

It didn't snow us in, but the weather was atrocious, horizontal gales and rain over Shap most days.

We didn't need the chicken or the pud as we had a wonderful Christmas Day with Jenny and Matthew and family in Kendal, and the next day we spent with Belinda and her new man near Windermere, and the next with our good friends in Grasmere.

It would have been more sensible to have rented a house nearer to them all, but the cabin was cosily warm, and driving down a different route each day meant seeing more of our beloved Lakes.

Never mind that the puppy was sick and had diarrhoea (thank goodness for the crate) and we had to go home via the vet.

The Alfrick Portakabin shop arrived in April—great excitement in the village—and needed a low loader lorry and a crane and some very skilful driving and manipulation to get it into the village hall car park. Before it could open the fifty or so volunteers had to attend Saturday meetings on health and hygiene, computer till lessons and first aid. I was pretty scornful about the necessity for the latter. Who on earth was going to collapse in the shop for goodness sake? Actually, it was me! I fainted while serving behind the counter, for no good reason and came home with a glorious technicolour black eye. Happily no one had to practice their mouth-to-mouth knowledge on me and I felt fine when I came round. I was the first and only entry in the accident book.

As there are always two people on at one time, and Richard and I decided on separate shifts, we have got to know many more people here and it is certainly keeping our brains active.

There has been a rather special art exhibition in Worcester, connected to our Dame Laura Knight Society. It is about her *en plein air* work and is a collection over two galleries one of which contains some of the paintings she did while staying in the Malvern area, including our own painting of *Plough Horses* which we inherited from The Wyke and had decided to lend to the exhibition. We took it down to the Penlee Gallery, Penzance, where the exhibition started. This was interesting in itself. We parked as near as we could to the gallery, only to get a £60 fine, but when I wrote to the council to explain, my cheque was returned with a very nice letter. No wonder I like Penzance.

The exhibition then travelled to Nottingham and finally to Worcester where our society had a private preview and were suitably impressed, especially by the huge painting of the Nuremburg trials which she did as official war artist.

Our holiday visiting the capitals of Eastern Europe by coach was not exactly enjoyable, but rather like reading a very good but harrowing book. By the time we had paid visits to Berlin, Warsaw, Krakow, Budapest, Vienna and Prague; seen films on the coach like *The Piano* and *The Boy in the Striped Pyjamas;* and been to Auschwitz, we were thoroughly steeped in the atrocities and the sorrows as well as the glorious buildings of each city.

The huge advantage was being looked after by excellent staff, hotels and no driving or flying. Much appreciated by us these days.

Interspersed with these events were more normal parts of life. Visits from family and friends throughout the year. Always welcomed and enjoyed. This included Oliver staying for a week. Now eleven, and Tristan, now thirteen, they were old enough and tall enough to sample something new: Go Ape in the Wyre Forest. I didn't realise that an adult was needed to accompany them in the tree tops and as I was unable to join them because my hip is still not very good, Richard did. I followed their progress sixty feet below, taking photos and chuckling to myself as the course got more and more difficult. The boys were very good at keeping an eye on Richard and checking his safety carabiners. There can't be many seventy-five-year-olds with Parkinson's who have been there and done that. Well done, Richard! The boys voted it 'brilliant'. I didn't tell their parents until they were safely home.

You may have heard or been told that Brian died in October. Though long expected, it was both sad and strange for me. We shared nineteen years and I bore his children with the utmost happiness. There doesn't seem to be any protocol for ex-wives, so I asked the 'children' to ask Fran if she would mind if I went to his funeral. She didn't mind and I was so glad I went, with Richard, whom I didn't know when Brian and I split up. All the family were there, even Barnaby, now in Nepal, and Natasha from Australia. All the grandchildren except for the two youngest were there too. As Brian had not given any ideas or suggestions about what he wanted, Fran and the family decided. Bryony and Barnaby gave eulogies at the traditional service in Wirksworth parish church, which was packed. He received wonderful obituaries in several of the papers he had worked on including, of course, the *Guardian*.

It certainly made me revise my wishes and to be precise about them, as I know it had at times been unnecessarily stressful for the family.

Brian's was not the only funeral this year and when a good friend dies it does affect one in all kinds of ways.

To cheer one up or drive one mad, get a puppy. Puzzle has fulfilled her remit superbly. It is good that she can be so sweet, so funny, so charming, and above all, that we love her. Because she has been the most disruptive, destructive, naughty, disobedient dog I have ever had. She can jump like a rocket, run like a rabbit, thieve like a professional, but would be a grand boy's dog, willing to join in anything—to the death if necessary. Some of the grandchildren love her, some scream like banshees when she appears. She loves (overwhelmingly loves) everybody. I exercise her with one of those throwing sticks and a ball so for every 3 steps that I take she runs about a hundred yards. She returns the ball to my feet so I don't even have to bend down. Marvellous. The other dogs find her a nuisance and the cats try hard to ignore her, which is incredibly difficult. I wish they would get their claws out sometimes and let her know they don't like being jumped on and licked to bits. I always thought I was quite good with dogs . . .

Enough, we are surviving—and if asked how we are, we say 'Fine, more or less.' I'm sure you know what we mean.

Hoping you are too. With love from us both.

Summer at Field End

Field End

Christmas 2013

Dear ———

A year of highs, lows, birthday parties, weddings, and alas, funerals.

Living in Alfrick has introduced us to a pretty full sociable life, from working in the shop about one afternoon a week and therefore meeting and getting to know (and remember their names) at least fifty people, to being in the drama group and unintentionally becoming the prompt for the play in April. Fun, but quite a commitment.

A few dinner parties became possible when an acquaintance started an enterprise to cater for parties etc., and she not only cooked and delivered the delicious food, but greeted the guests and washed up as well, so we were all happy, especially me.

On coach trips from here I have been to Chatsworth Christmas Fair, Adam Henson's farm (featured on *Countryfile* every week), and with Richard we spent two nights in Whitby with the Dame Laura Knight Society exploring Staithes where she lived and painted before living in Cornwall—you might have seen the film *Summer in February*, and we also went to the National Portrait Gallery in London to see the exhibition on her work there.

We took part in a Safari Supper, entertaining eight people to a starter and then we all moved on to different houses for different courses, meeting different people and then all fifty of us meeting up for coffee in a larger house. So successful it may be repeated.

One of the main events for me happened in February when Barnaby asked me if I would take his two children to Geneva at half term as he was travelling there from New York—where he moved earlier this year—as part of his job for the UN.

We would all stay in a flat (not a hotel as I had rather hoped) and I would entertain the children all day while he worked, and

I would make the meals, etc. I was delighted to do this as I now see them so seldom. By airport taxi, Easyjet and a Geneva bus (Barnaby was unable to meet us off the plane) we arrived at the flat and I even shopped on the way for supper. Both Sacha and Jamie (ten and twelve) speak French so we managed, although in the four days there none of us sussed out the transport system and ended up not even trying to pay on the buses, but ready to show complete ignorance if challenged (not difficult).

On the first evening when the children were in bed, Barnaby said he had something to tell me. He said, 'I'm getting married and we want you to come to the wedding.' Me, after deep breath, 'Oh. Marvellous, yes, of course I'll come—who is she?' Barnaby, ignoring the question, 'It's in New York.' Me, thinking of all the problems. 'Oh, fantastic! When is it?'

Barnaby, 'Next week.' Me, 'What!' Barnaby, 'And you mustn't tell anybody.' Me, 'But Richard—he'll want to know why I'm off again across the world—I can't leave him without telling him why.' Barnaby, 'Well, just him then, not the family.'

He wanted to tell the children and Chantal first, but break it to them as gently as possible and not suddenly. He has been divorced for over a year and his bride is Vietnamese, thirty-four, never been married and met him in the UN in Ha Noi. She lived in the UK for a year when younger and speaks very good English and, as we all know now, is a lovely person, and they appear extremely happy.

So I flew to New York for two nights, just like one of those businessmen one reads about flitting all over the world, and was the only witness at their wedding in a civil ceremony in a huge hall where a hundred couples waited in queues to get married. Hai Dzung and Barnaby have spent nearly a week here with us recently. The children spent a fortnight with them in New York at half term and she looked after them in the daytime while he worked. She has now got a job with the UN there, as hoped, and they have moved into a flat of their own on Roosevelt Island. The only worry is that on one of his many flights these days he had a deep vein thrombosis and spent eleven hours in Geneva hospital, and is now on pills and injections before he flies.

I have just returned from a workshop in Worcester with Jenny, Matthew's wife, on foetal alcohol spectrum; their adopted daughter is affected, so it was particularly interesting, with a very good speaker who has two affected children, and is trying to make it better known as ignorance is widespread and the damage to babies in the womb is far greater than drugs, and it is mainly adoptee parents who are trying to get help. There was one woman there who had drunk during pregnancy herself and now had two affected children. She cried.

The second wedding was also family, my youngest nephew, Jacob married Claire in the village in the Yorkshire Dales where they were children. The drive there, the setting of the village hall and the adjoining hay field (uncut) were magical. We sat on straw bales for the ceremony and the wind threatened to blow a magnificent sycamore tree down on to us as the happy couple processed down an avenue of wild flowers.

We caught up with all the news (always so good to see my sister and her family) and left for a week in a remote one-room bothy near Devoke Water in the Lake District.

We travelled from there to see old friends almost every day (good) which meant going on scary roads that we used to skim over without a qualm (bad).

The other holiday, never to be forgotten, was spent on the Monmouth and Brecon canal in a narrowboat with Tristan (fifteen), Carenza (twelve) and, perish the thought, the dog Puzzle.

I took three books to read and imagined relaxing, eating at picturesque pubs every evening, and of course it would be sunny.

Within two minutes Puzzle had fallen in, and Tristan followed shortly after. The loo was only a foot off the ground, impossible for a bad hip (as some will know!) and Richard had to kneel to pee, and got cramp as he went down. The young enjoyed it, but the old were completely stressed out after the first day. And I never even opened a book. And it drizzled continually. And the pubs were either closed, not dog friendly, or too far away.

For sad times, among them have been the death of our gentle lurcher Daisy, age not known as she was a rescue dog, but about twelve, and three good friends, much missed. Funerals are now as varied as weddings, and always memorable and so moving.

The birthdays were celebrated in a marvellous old manor house in Devon—cousins Mike and Hilda, both eighty—and in St Giles House, Oxford—grandson Rowan aged four, as Natasha and George were back for a holiday from Australia. Wonderful locations and happy families.

But finally, there was The Book. *Morning Has Broken. Written and* illustrated by me. After thirty-three years I published my book, the diary I wrote when I first worked at Bowood when I was employed as the relief milker for the five hundred cows on the estate, in four separate herds. Richard was my boss and had twenty-four men working for him—and me. It is an account of my life during the four seasons and how I coped with it all, the hours, my children, and the very steep learning curve (and Richard!).

A local family firm published it and reactions have been amazingly complimentary, so I am pleased (to say the least). I have been asked if there will be the next instalment, but no, that is it. It was a unique experience and nothing could equal it. I now feel I could die happy.

We continue to mutually discuss health issues with anyone interested, but I won't go into all that, so please have a happy and healthy Christmas and New Year. We'll be thinking of you, with love from us both.

The sitting room at Field End

Field End

Christmas 2014

Dear ——

If I didn't keep a diary I would never remember the happenings of this year. These have been many and varied. We were lucky not to be seriously affected by the floods and power cuts over the Christmas period. Our turkey was not ruined as we didn't have one, but the combination of rain and mud and two dogs right into February made us truly thankful when spring came at last.

For Richard's Christmas and birthday present I bought a beautiful nearly life size nude statue for the garden, known now as Winter Jasmine, who gives us a lot of pleasure.

We had a party for the Dame Laura Knight Society Committee, using our local catering wonder woman and in April went on a coach tour of A. J. Munnings country (Suffolk) with them and steeped ourselves in his glorious paintings.

Coach trips to London; Bletchley Park; two nights at WI Denman College for silk painting; and a week in Malta (surprisingly successful and possibly our last abroad) have all been stimulating and stressless. Going by train to Silverdale to stay with my sister before we all went to Jenny's very enjoyable fiftieth birthday bash was less good. Manoeuvring Richard on and off trains and between platforms was rather taxing! Driving is now pretty much up to me.

I was asked to paint a picture as a gift to the Suckley Parish Council chairman to celebrate his fifty years in that office! I enjoyed depicting various areas of his life over that time.

I am sculpting Carenza's head at the moment, with the help of our seventy-nine-year-old tutor who is good at solving problems like cracks and holes in the cast which shouldn't be there.

My reading group continues to be a joy and we laugh a lot which is good for us all, aged from sixty-five to ninety-five.

In June we joined the Alfrick Open Gardens Day, held biannually, for the first and probably the last time. Preparing for it was hard work but, as we had 130 visitors, it was worth it.

The event raises money for local charities. We had hoped to go round some of the other gardens but we were too busy.

Partly because of that event I decided I needed a gardener. Richard did not want anyone on his territory, no problem. Andrew, a fit young Polish man, comes for two hours a fortnight and does the jobs I no longer can or want to do. We also now employ a window cleaner who sprays the glass with special water—no soap or drips—and he will do the gutters and white fascia boards as Richard shouldn't be climbing ladders, although as I write this he is up one trimming a climbing rose.

He has given up the footpath wardening, partly because his 'mate' has had a knee replacement and I don't think it is a good idea for him to be doing it on his own now. He walks the dog for an hour every morning and still keeps fit, sings and goes to music appreciation, but Parkinson's is affecting him more. He no longer wishes to go to the theatre or cinema, so I go by myself or with friends.

We drove to the Lakes in August, swapping houses with Jenny and Matthew in Kendal, and seeing old friends while there. This worked well.

I also drove to Anglesey recently to see Ann, my sister, whose husband died shortly after they moved there. Inoperable cancer was found only days after they arrived and they had a truly nightmare time, especially as they found the house was absolutely filthy and so full of left behind things that they couldn't unpack. Their family rallied brilliantly and took over the cleaning and supporting, and even cutting down trees and gardening. Jack did not want a funeral so (like my father) they are organising a gathering, but in Langdale, and will scatter his ashes at the top of Jack's Rake, the climb he did on his eightieth birthday! If you know the Lakes you will appreciate that achievement.

The road to Anglesey from here was spectacular, through Wales with the autumn colours and superb scenery. I like Anglesey very much, as we have had three good holidays there. Ann's eldest son lives a couple of miles away, so she is not alone and has just acquired two delightful kittens to add to the dog, cat and tortoise she already has, and she is planning to have hens in the spring. After talking solidly for two days and laughing quite a lot, I felt she would be all right, despite the very traumatic and sad experience. Richard's son Will stayed with him here.

Just as well, as soon after I returned he had a strange and alarming episode which we think now was a urinary infection. An immediate visit to the GP resulted in antibiotics which gradually brought him back to where he was before it happened. As the doctor alerted the early intervention for dementia team, we then had a visit from two women (Mel and Hel!) and they assessed him and made an appointment for a CT scan in January.

We have already gone through the procedure of power of attorney so that is sorted, written our wills, belong to Dignity in Dying and can now enjoy ourselves as best we can.

Especially as I was diagnosed with breast cancer in late July. I had a lumpectomy in August and apart from having to travel to three hospitals in two consecutive days to have the necessary tests, treatments and operation, the care I received from the NHS was wonderful. Helped, I think, by my surgeon, a rather dishy (Richard's opinion) youngish man whose spell I immediately fell under. To my surprise, I did not feel worried or frightened at all and certainly not about dying. As I was told I was clear I opted out of the radiotherapy. However, here I still am!

We have seen much more of Barnaby this year as he stays with us every time he comes over from New York to see his children, on his way to or from Geneva. So we see them too when he brings them here. I had thought of flying to New York when their baby was born (in November) but this is no longer sensible. He and Hai Dzung stayed for a few days in the summer so we got to know her better, which was lovely. The photo of the baby, born two weeks early and while Jamie and Sacha were still staying with them over their half term (all somewhat dramatic!) is very sweet, so they saw him too, which I am sure was good.

After Bryony's old ex-guide dog died this year, she decided a small, easy to manage lapdog type would be sensible. Truffle is a curly cuddly bichon frise and is indeed adorable, but also *very* feisty. His behaviour has caused a number of problems, not least barking all night and causing the death by chasing of two guinea pigs and a rabbit, all of which used to have a very pleasant free range life in the garden. So Bryony has called in a police dog trainer to help! I didn't feel able to offer advice as Puzzle is still no advert for my training skills. In fact, Belinda, who was staying with us recently, said, 'If I get a dog, it won't be one like her!'

We wish you a happy Christmas and a *very good year*, (never mind the *new*).

With love from us both.

Winter walk in Alfrick

Field End

Christmas 2015

Dear ——

This Christmas letter is no ordinary letter. It has not been an easy year, and culminated in Richard taking his own life at the end of September, discussing his intention beforehand with our families. He wanted to prevent the possibility of being a burden because of the increasing effects of Parkinson's and the onset of dementia. He was not depressed and was in his right mind. He was very sure that he did not want to go into care. All the family understood and supported him. I told him I would be with him to the end.

Many of you reading this will know this already. I received many, many beautiful cards and tributes to him with moving words of support. (If yours was among them, thank you so much, they are a great comfort to me. I would like to reply to them all, but this would take some time.)

The gathering to remember Richard was held in Alfrick village hall (after a private family cremation) to which all his children and my children came, with Penny and Barbara, and cousins and sister, and seven of the twelve grandchildren, as well as many friends from near and far. It was a most memorable occasion. He recorded his own voice on his life two years ago while his voice was still strong, and which he said was fulfilled and happy.

Natasha came from Texas to stay and help, and created a photoboard with photos of Richard over his seventy-eight years, showing his many interests and abilities from farming to making chairs in the woods, to his keep fit class, the choir, the footpath wardening, and all our happy holidays by caravan, boat, plane, train and car. There was an amusing one of him taking part in *The Full Monty* on the Grasmere stage.

Barnaby from New York and Matthew from Kendal stayed

with me in turn to sort the mounds of paperwork that my brain would not take in. Bryony was a very sympathetic rock in the background, always there in spirit. Between them all they kept me going and were the greatest help.

Although suicide is no longer a crime, it appears that being with a dearly loved husband to the end of his life and not stopping him *is*, so the police and coroner and statements have been involved, with the possibility of prosecution for breaking the law. I knew I must not assist him, but I knew nothing of the crime of negligence and manslaughter! So have been under considerable stress, only recently removed, as not being in the public interest.

The most frequent comment made about Richard was, 'He was a lovely man' and indeed he was *My Lovely Man* and I miss him dreadfully, but he made his decision and I believe he was brave and thoughtful and I supported him wholeheartedly in life and death.

There is to be an inquest in February. All this has not made life any easier, but I am coping with the kind and generous help of family and friends.

During the past year there were good times and pleasurable outings, a week in the Lake District to join my sister and family for the scattering of her husband's ashes in the most beautiful place by Elterwater, and followed by Richard taking Belinda, Sophie and Trinley (Will)—Nicola was not able to be there—up to the place behind Windy Ridge where he wanted his ashes scattered (and which will be done when Trinley comes out of his year retreat in the Arran Buddhist Centre).

Our last day out was to a ploughing match held on a local farm. He put on his cap, his wellies and took his crook and mingled with the farmers and the tractors, for that was where his heart was and always has been.

With love,
Rosemary.